WORKING
WHILE BLACK

WORKING WHILE BLACK

THE BLACK PERSON'S GUIDE TO SUCCESS IN THE WHITE WORKPLACE

MICHELLE T. JOHNSON

Lawrence Hill Books

Library of Congress Cataloging-in-Publication Data

Johnson, Michelle T.
    Working while black : the black person's guide to success in the white
workplace / Michelle T. Johnson.— 1st ed.
        p. cm.
    Includes bibliographical references and index.
    ISBN 1-55652-510-9
    1. African Americans—Employment—Psychological aspects.
2. Success in business. I. Title.
HD8081.A65J64 2004
650.1′089′96073—dc21

                                                    2003011630

Contact the author at MTJOHNLAW@aol.com to share your
working-world experiences.

■

Cover and interior design: Monica Baziuk

Published by Lawrence Hill Books
An imprint of Chicago Review Press, Incorporated
814 North Franklin Street
Chicago, Illinois 60610
ISBN 1-55652-510-9
Printed in the United States of America
5   4   3   2   1

■

This book is dedicated to all the ancestors who made the opportunities possible, and to the descendants who endure and made the book necessary to write.

■

CONTENTS

■

ACKNOWLEDGMENTS

■

SPECIAL THANKS TO my Muse, Bootsie, Peaches, Woo Woo, and Professor Shutter Bug (commonly known as Cherry Muhanji, Adrienne Bennett, LaSandra Pearl, Quan Tracy Cherry, and Sam Upshaw, Jr.). Unlimited gratitude to family members Cliffie Owens, Ethel Johnson, and the infamous Hilbert Ray, as well as all ancestors who got me here, particularly Fannie Estell McCrary Stapleton and James Owens.

Additional thanks to J. Eric Durr, Wade Kerrigan, and Jessica Kerrigan for their concrete and invaluable help.

Special thanks to Yuval Taylor and Lisa Rosenthal, my editors, who kept the train on the track.

Particular thanks to the people who provided the inspiration—both negative and positive—for the examples in this book.

DISCLAIMER

Every incident, person, and example in this book is either a true story or based on a true story. Because of the nature of my job as a mediator and former employment attorney in a law firm (and because I have friends and associates who will hunt me down and beat me for telling their business), real names are not used and, when necessary, identifying details are changed to protect privacy.

This is *not*, repeat *not*, legal advice. Please do not let any comments in this book serve as your sole or motivating basis for doing or saying anything that will have legal ramifications. If you really think you've got a problem, talk to a friend, a counselor, a spiritual adviser, or an attorney and get advice from a professional who knows the specific facts of your situation. Refer to the resources in the back of this book for further assistance and inspiration.

INTRODUCTION

■

RACE IS PROBABLY one of the trickiest subjects two people can talk about. It's particularly tricky when the two people are of two different races, because their perspectives are so ingrained they can't really get inside the other person's head.

That's why the times we live in are so amazingly contradictory. We can sit in front of a tiny little screen, click a few buttons, type a few words, and have access to information from the other side of the globe in a matter of seconds; yet, as a black person in America, you could spend hours at a party talking with a white person about the reasons why it is acceptable for black people to use the word *nigger* but not whites. That is because information and understanding are not synonymous.

Working While Black is a black person's guide to employment in the white work world. That seems like a simple topic, and yet it implies and promises so much. It implies that in a few easy steps, I can tell you how to navigate the work world as a black person. Well, I can't—I'm still navigating that myself.

One thing I can tell you is that being a black person in the white work world is about having internal fortitude. There are no easy steps. There are no simple answers. Each person is completely different, each job raises different challenges, and each step of the process calls for different skills.

In an ideal world, this book would simply be about employment, and a person of any race could pick it up and get every concept in it. It would just be a book about how to pick a career, how to get a job, and how to keep and enjoy a job. There wouldn't be any special considerations. But this is the real world and so there are.

I was told that this book shouldn't be too negative because young blacks would suffer from a lack of motivation. What my well-meaning white friend did not get is that motivation is not the issue. Black people are going to be highly motivated in whatever we do. We're going to reach for the stars and try to get ours no matter what because that is who we are. We're human, and we want to live well and do well, too. Blacks get inundated with the same mass advertising that white America gets—taunting us to want more, buy more, own better. Most people buying this book aren't going to succumb to a life of crime or purposeful unemployment just because the working life is hard.

A book, like a life, is a work in progress—especially when you are writing a book about something that touches your life profoundly, both personally and professionally.

While I worked on this book I tried to focus on specific points and my mind became flooded with half-forgotten memories of examples from my own life addressing what I was trying to say. Some detail from a case that supported my point would come back to me, or I'd recall a situation in a friend's life that was particularly illustrative.

In the same week I sent my finished manuscript to my editor, one of my closest friends, a black professional, was fired from her job semi-suddenly, and, in my job as an attorney, I sat through the depositions of four black employees suing their company for race discrimination.

During this same week I was reading a book that suggested we attract every experience and condition we have in life because of our feelings, including particular issues such as illness, tragedy, and discrimination.

The point about attracting everything that happens to us, good or bad, was a bit surreal. The concept went against everything I've ever thought about bad things happening to good people, and yet totally supported the concept, too. For example, while my initial emotional reaction to my friend being fired was to wail about how terribly unfair it was and how screwed I felt she had been, she was the first to say that while she was nervous about finding a job in a stalled economy, she was relieved to some degree because of how much she hated her job. So, in a sense, she was an example of how deep-rooted negativity about a situation can attract the one thing you think you don't want.

As I sat in the plaintiffs' depositions in the case, I was amazed at the degree of fresh, sincere passion these people expressed in recounting events that had happened years before. Even though the supervisors they complained about were no longer with the company, even though most of them had moved on to better jobs, and even though all of them sounded like they had good lives outside of work, they still swelled with anger and indignation as they talked about their experiences.

The concept of attracting experience is equally relevant here. While these people may not have deserved bad treatment at the hands of either illegal discrimination or garden-variety (yet legal) racism, in some part they were equal parties to their pain. I don't mean they were responsible for being on the receiving end of their alleged discrimination, but that they were choosing to stay stuck in the pain of the experience by constantly reliving it through the lawsuit. It's like the Buddhist concept: Pain is a necessary part of life, but suffering is optional.

It becomes a very tough statement to make, because it seems as if we are letting our oppressors off the hook. Failing to blame and accuse and attack bad behavior feels as if you're endorsing it. I think this is one of the reasons why blacks (in general) and whites (in general) have such different views of affirmative action. Many blacks, in supporting affirmative action, are saying, "Hey, white folks, you don't need to be off the hook yet. The playing field hasn't even begun to be even and to say otherwise is to let you get away with all you've done, all you're still doing, and all you're going to do." The whites who oppose affirmative action, on the other hand, are saying, "Look, black people, you can't have it both ways. You say you don't want decisions to be about race when it hurts you, but you're willing to let decisions be about race when it helps you. That's not fair to the hard-working, innocent white people who have not committed any wrongs."

I'm writing this book because I've had the full-time job and joy of being black for 38 years. For eight of those years, I've been a full-time lawyer, mostly practicing in employment law, and since the age of 14 I have consistently been either a part-time or a full-time member of America's labor force.

As an employee, I wish I had a five-dollar bill for every time I have had to examine how a comment, a decision, or something else done by a white coworker or boss might have had negative implications. I've even had conversations with white coworkers who also found themselves scratching their heads, puzzled over the stupidity of a white boss who left racial tracks behind.

Sometimes that Monday morning conversation, question, or analysis involved some backstabbing maneuver done by a member of our own race. Yep, I mean black-on-black crime in the workplace. Every time that little problem comes up, your fellow brother or sister's knife seems just a little sharper and plunges a little deeper into your heart.

Race is the little angel/devil that constantly hovers over your shoulder in the work world if you're a black person. If you're particularly blessed or lucky there may be entire weeks of your working life where you can get so immersed in the pleasures and satisfaction your job gives you that you can have a fade out and not consider racial implications. I don't mean fade out and forget you're black, but rather not be any more aware of being black than you are when you're at home, or at a family reunion, or driving in a car by yourself.

Whites really don't want to hear this. I think it is because part of them feels guilty, and another part of them gets angry for feeling guilty about something that they don't think they should feel guilty about because it's not their fault, and the cycle starts again. Oh, well. This book isn't about white people's responses. It is about black empowerment in a world where we do have to deal with white people's responses.

I had my first job at age 14. Because I was blessed with a womanly physique (to put it tactfully), the fast food restaurant manager didn't blink when I said I was 16 years old. I honestly can't remember if it was the manager's suggestion or my own to leave, but I know I didn't last in that first job for more than three weeks. What I do distinctly remember about the job was my strong belief that people needed to be given two packets of syrup when they ordered pancakes for breakfast. The manager insisted that people only needed one. Even then, I had an oddball sense of integrity. I lied about my age to the get the job (my first and only resume fraud), but I was willing to lose the job because I didn't think it was fair that people found out only after they got home that they had way more pancakes than syrup.

But the job you have at 14, to make money for stuff you don't really need, is a far different reality than the job you have at 21, when you live 2,000 miles from home and your college degree is so new it sparkles. At 21 you not only have rent, food, and student loans at stake, you also have ego. Therefore, when your first job out of college ends with your boss, in my case an East Coast city editor, telling another reporter that he didn't like me because "she doesn't act grateful enough to be here," well, you know it's going to be a long and bumpy ride. Actually, in that particular case it was a short and bumpy ride.

I learned a lot from that experience. I learned that no matter how good you are at what you do, if you've got a white boy attitude in a black woman's body, there's going to be a lot of clinking and clashing at some point. I also learned that how you succeed in the workplace is often about how you manage the workplace itself *and* how well you do your job.

When I buy a good self-help book, I hope it gives me a fresh look at a particular part of my life. But I don't expect a book to substitute for my own decision-making process.

If you're reading this book, you're probably a black person who's working. You have a job, or you want a job, or you've just lost a job and you want to know if you're holding it together right. Since every job is so distinctly different, you should use this book as a guide to trusting your own inner light. For example, for a black person, getting a job as a nurse's aide in Tupelo, Mississippi, will be handled differently from getting one in Boise, Idaho. While most of the essentials are the same—the application and interview process—the nuances might be completely different. The supervisor in Boise might be indifferent to whether you are black or not, while the top dog in Tupelo, because of his history with blacks, might be a straight-up racist. While this book may provide some guidelines on what to do about getting past the racist, only the person applying for the job knows whether that would be in his or her best interest anyway.

How you start is how you finish. In starting off any job or job situation with questions instead of assumptions, you end up with more peace of mind and have a better foundation for your decisions.

This book doesn't try to come up with the Holy Grail of answers. The goal is to help you increase your awareness. While certain realities might not change, increased awareness might help you make better on-the-spot decisions when you're at work. On many days, the decision may be nothing more than choosing not to internalize a dose of someone else's bad behavior.

Knowing your intention is in your hands. Choosing your options is in your hands. Helping you to evaluate your options is the aim of this book. Among these pages you'll find information on:

- Why blacks need to think of the workplace differently, and with a strategy
- How to decide where to work (the internal process you need to go through)

- How to get the first job, or how to career hop (once you decide what you want, how to get it)

- The importance of language and grooming style in the workplace

- Alliances in the workplace

- Fitting in without selling out

- Attitude issues that arise in the workplace if you're black

- Considering legal options when problems arise

- What happens when you get fired or quit

- How to be a healthy, happy person inside and outside of work

In the year 2000, 49 percent of the employees filing claims of racial discrimination in California were black. Considering that California is one of five states with the largest black population, that's indicative that black employees all over are feeling the need for guidance while wading through the white workplace.

There are employment manuals, and there are books that describe the sociological experience of being a black person in America. *Working While Black* aims to combine both—it's an employment guide that acknowledges the average black reader's frustration about working in a society where equality is a promise but not a reality.

WORKING WHILE BLACK

1

THE 15 PERCENT DIFFERENCE

■

LIFE IS HARD FOR BLACKS before they get their first job. Whether we went to a private school or a public school or an all-black school or a mostly white school, if we've dealt with whites, in any capacity, being different and having different experiences isn't new to us. Today's average 16-year-old black may deal with it less than his grandparents did when they were 16 years old, but less than is not the same as not at all.

What I think many whites, including (ironically) even liberal whites, don't get, is that even though our experiences as black people can be 85 percent the same as white people, some days that 15 percent difference is the only difference we feel.[1] Technically,

---

1 Please understand that the phrase "15 percent difference" is neither scientific nor factual. It's merely shorthand to address the fact that as a black employee in white America, most of the objective things you deal with are not race issues. Also, please do not feel that I'm saying that the 15 percent difference is only a minor aspect of the work experience. For some people, it's the most influential aspect of who they are. For example, a Condoleezza Rice has to worry less about the 15 percent difference when she's contemplating foreign

much of this book will apply to any worker, regardless of race, but that 15 percent difference for blacks is going to put just a little bit of a spin on the rest of our day.

For example, applying for a job is applying for a job—no matter what your color or race, you need to fill out an application or submit a resume and go through some formalized process to actually get the job offer. But at some point, there are those 15 percent issues that put just a little twist on our experience as blacks trying to get a job. For example, if the receptionist who takes your application has had bad experiences with blacks, your resume may end up at the bottom of the pile, meaning you never even get the interview. Therefore, that 15 percent can be the difference between you getting through the door or not, and the difference between you being happy or miserable once you get through that door.

This book aims to do a couple of things. One is to address the 85 percent commonality, and two is to give you helpful advice, tips, and perspective for when that 15 percent perspective pops up. I know that many times just knowing that I'm not alone is enough to get through an experience or put perspective on a puzzling situation.

---

policy in Russia than she did with her first job out of college. It's not that Ms. Rice doesn't deal with the 15 percent issues any more, they just play out differently when you and the President of the United States watch football games together. I'm sure that when Condoleezza talks behind closed doors with her girls about earlier jobs, she could write a book about how her 15 percent issues played out less than positively. Jesse Jackson, on the other hand, has to constantly factor in the black perspective in what he does just by the nature of his particular career path. Condoleezza is no less black than Jesse. It's just that on most days, as one of the single most important black people in government, she gets to leverage her 15 percent differently than Jesse does. One could say that when you're a leader in the civil rights movement, your 15 percent is actually 100 percent.

When I was in law school, many of the other blacks I met there wanted to go into civil rights law because they wanted to make a difference in the lives of black people. While civil rights law is a great area, I personally feel that black people make a difference wherever we are and whatever we do. We pay taxes. We have wills and estates when we die. We get divorced. We have car accidents. We buy and sell companies. In other words, as blacks we have the power to influence the whole world. One black person changes the dynamic just by being in the room; so yes, while it is important to be at the forefront of civil rights, all these other areas of the law need us, too. One of the reasons our people marched for civil rights and put their bodies and lives and livelihoods at risk was so that no door would be closed to us. One of my favorite quotes from Martin Luther King, Jr., speaks to this issue:

> *If you are called to be a street sweeper, sweep streets even as Michelangelo painted, or Beethoven composed music, or Shakespeare wrote poetry. Sweep streets so well that all the hosts of heaven and earth will pause to say, "Here lived a great street sweeper who did his job well."*

Notice that King didn't say if you're called to be a doctor, lawyer, or chemical engineer. King said a street sweeper because he knew that it was a humble job but one that still required heart to do it well. I'd like to think that one of King's points was that the struggle for equality was not just for black Americans to get the best jobs in our society but rather for each of us to get *any* job or opportunity in our society that was best suited to our individual dream.

Maybe that's why it is easier to be a black civil rights attorney than a black tax attorney in a large, white law firm, or maybe it's easier to be a teacher in an inner-city school district rather than headmaster at a hoity-toity East Coast school. But each person has the right to deal with that 15 percent difference however he or she chooses. Maybe the black tax attorney gets her rocks off from calculating tax exemptions for the wealthy. Maybe the black headmaster loves a more extravagant lifestyle than a public school salary can offer. Therefore, when these 15 percent issues come up, it may all be worth it. It should be, because none of us can avoid it anyway.

Let me repeat: *none of us can avoid it anyway.* No matter what path you choose, if another person can look at you and tell you're black, that will mold your experience with that person from that point forward. Notice I didn't say negatively mold, just shape.

Do You Instinctively Aim to Survive, Strive, or Thrive?

My observation, from 24 years of working and 8 years of practicing employment law, is that black folks have roughly one of three instinctive agendas in the workplace. And this delineation is true whether we're talking minimum wage, blue-collar, just plain-ol'-shirt-on-your-back-when-you-go-to-work-in-the-morning collar, or white-collar professional.[2]

---

2 My classification does not cover artists, athletes, or entrepreneurs, or even blacks who work for other blacks. (However, I do like black opera singer Leontyne Price's advice: "Be black, shine, aim high.") Now while blacks who work for other blacks have similar issues and dynamics as blacks who work for whites, this situation still raises other issues. For

Working while black requires you to have a mental awareness, a psychological game plan, so to speak. You've got to know if you're in it just to survive, if you're in for the strive—to get ahead—or if you're in it to thrive and be your natural brown self and make the white folks move to your rhythm instead of you constantly having to adapt to theirs.

There is no particular mentality that is best for every black person. Every job change, every career choice, and maybe even every change in supervision might force you to make a drastic shift in whether you're in the game to survive, to strive, or to thrive; however, no matter what your initial motivation or instinct, you can always choose to be a driver, creating your own destiny.

I've created these categories based on my experiences in the working world.

For me, there is no value judgment attached to being in the workplace as a survivor, a striver, or a thriver. We've all been visitors to each place at some point in our working career. Some people settle into the lifelong comfort zone of being a survivor. Some people were ambitious from the first step they took as a toddler, so they will be diehard strivers. Other people come out of the womb pushing their mama's limits and those thrivers spend the rest of their lives doing the same to everyone else's limits.

---

example, a friend of mine, an attorney who once worked for an all-black law firm, and I used to trade many a long-distance phone call with stories about who had it rougher. In our game of "who's got it worse," we would compare insanities of kowtowing to white folks versus working for black folks trippin' because they pull the strings. We jokingly decided to stop playing that game when we realized we were always going to stalemate, since at the end of the day we both worked for bosses who left us needing to have this conversation in the first place.

A *survivor* is there for the paycheck and lives his or her work life like a duck floating on smooth waters. Someone who is trying to survive wants to be under the radar screen. His goal is to not draw attention to himself or do anything other than work, collect the paycheck, and get out the door when the clock strikes whenever. Survivors do not like negative attention. They do not like positive attention. They don't like any attention and are indifferent to the desire to distinguish themselves.

There is a black woman I've known all of my adult life. She's been my mentor, my boss, my guide, my lookout, my savior, and always my friend. Years before I knew I would become a lawyer or write a book (or even believed I could do either), she was the original person to teach me by example how to be a survivor, a striver, and the ultimate thriver. Now she's in her late 50s, and she has one of the best descriptions I can think of for what it is to be in the workplace on the survivor agenda. As she puts it now, "You get to the point where you're just in it for the health insurance."

Being a survivor as a black person in the workplace can mean different things to different people at different points in their lives. It's the person who knows this particular boss can't stand her and is looking for any excuse to eliminate her job. It's the person who is working the only job he can find that pays more than $5 an hour because he has a family to support. It's the person who has put his 30 years in and knows he's gone as far as he is going to get in an organization before retirement hits.

A *striver* likes the radar screen. She wants to be on it, but only if it's a good thing. If she's lucky, she aims to *run* the radar screen one day, even if no black employee in the history of her workplace has ever done it before. The black striver wants acclaim, promotions, and success. She wants to play the game because she believes she can win. She doesn't mind hearing about glass ceilings because, in her mind, glass can be broken. She sees to the top and doesn't care if she bumps her head or gets scraped on the climb.

A striver is one who believes that the system works and believes that benefits come by following the system. Look at newly minted black college graduates and that is probably where you are going to see the prototype of a striver. They believe that an education, a plan, and pure, raw ambition will make the difference. These folks strive forward, strive to the top, strive to get a huge slice of what their parents may not necessarily have had a shot at.

The *thriver* is the black person who not only dances to his or her own beat, but also creates his or her own rhythm. Thrivers don't care about the radar screen because they figure the radar screen was invented to track other people anyway, not them. Thrivers are the ones who are going to dress the way they want, talk the way they want, and it is not an option for them to get in by trying to fit in.

Thrivers are easy to spot. The thriver is the black person who puts the white folks either a little on edge or a lot on edge. White bosses assume (sometimes mistakenly, sometimes not) that if any black employee might file a complaint or sue them, it will be the thriver. Of course, bosses don't refer to them as thrivers, but more likely as "troublemakers" or "the mouthy ones" or "the ones with an attitude problem." A thriver may just be the person referred to by name with an accompanying eye roll. Success for the thriver isn't necessarily the goal the way it is for a striver, although some are quite successful. Some are loud. Others are offbeat. The truly lucky ones work at places where they are not perceived as loud or different or ghetto or crazy or a troublemaker or any of the

other negative labels that often get attached to blacks who operate by their own internal agendas.

My woman friend whom I mentioned earlier as an example
of someone in the survivor mode as she cruises toward the next
stage of her life, was an unabashed thriver when I first met her
15 years ago. She was the person who taught me how to have a
"F—k You Fund" at all times so that if your employer ever
tripped too hard, you could say "F—k you," quit without a job,
and have a three-month cushion to find a job where you won't
get disrespected. I can't say I've always had a fund that size, but
I did inherit the attitude.

The Proof Is in the Pudding

Being black in America isn't simple, and going to work every day
as a black person is not for the faint-hearted. A few years ago, I
made up this saying. It is a silly, nonsensical expression that I liked
and it's stuck with a few friends: "The proof is in the pudding,
not the pudding mix." That was my standard way of saying look
to someone's results and not just what she says about how she is
going to get the results. Being black in America isn't simple, but
it is simple to constantly evaluate your circumstances to make
sure you're achieving what you want, because that's the pudding—coming up with a work experience that makes you feel
happy and successful. Unless you're rich, you work for yourself,
or you're a homemaker, you have to work for someone else. Let's
face it, even if you work for yourself or you work for other blacks,
you still need to figure out how to deal with whites in the work
context, whether it's customers, clients, vendors, employees, the

government—you name it. The proof is in the pudding, not the pudding mix.

This book doesn't provide fill-in-the-blank answers. (I wish I had those kinds of answers because I could have used them myself over the years.) This book attempts to ask good questions, outline common-sense scenarios, and aims to provide real-life solutions. My division between blacks on whether they are in it to survive, strive, or thrive is by no means definitive. It's just a shorthand way of explaining the different approaches that black employees take when managing the workplace jungle.

A white male friend of mine recently talked about a mutual friend of ours who is a white woman and disabled. She has been in a wheelchair her entire adult life. My male friend commented that in terms of life difficulties, it is probably harder for our friend who is white than for those faced with racial discrimination, because her limitations are physical. I pointed out that in some ways it's probably the opposite because ultimately, as difficult as her situation is, no one is going to argue with her about whether she can go up stairs or through a door. Her disability is a physical fact, so she doesn't have to explain or doubt herself. Ultimately, no one blames her for being upset if she can't enter a building or use a bathroom. When you're talking limitations relating to race, you never know what's really going on (unless a person uses the *nigger* word, which is something even the stupidest white person knows not to do in public anymore). You can feel resistance or insensitivity or futility sometimes, but you can't see it or prove it. The existence of a physical limitation doesn't have to be explained. When a person is blind, for example, and walks into another person accidentally, no one speculates whether the person is just clumsy or has a defective cane. But if black people say they received bad service at a restaurant because of their race, some white people usually rush in to offer their own bad experiences at the same restaurant, or speculate that maybe the server might have been having a bad day. My point is not that it is better to be physically disabled than black (and I won't touch on the difficulties of being both), but that to be black in working white America is to have your experiences constantly negated and challenged by whites who can't understand or don't want to understand. Part of this understanding is to remember that if the average black person is wrong some of the time when he says race is an issue, then that means that some of the time he's right. If there is anything more stressful to a black person than sensing something is about race when you can't really know for sure, it's having a white person act like you're blameworthy to even consider whether race is an issue.

If you're a reasonable person, you know that just because you feel something is off does not necessarily mean that it is about race. But sometimes you just don't know. Again, that 15 percent factor constantly creeps up.

Most of the time, you never really know. Hopefully, what you get from reading this book is the comfort of knowing that it is OK to not always know, and that on those occasions when you question, questions are good because the path to finding out what you need to know can be as useful as the answer you come up with.

The advice-giving books (also known as "self-help" and "how-to") still leap off the shelves. We all want to know the exact steps to take to make our lives better. I know I've bought several dozen in my life on how to lose weight, gain a relationship, obtain a job, unload a bad habit, and more. I'm a particular fan of the "Idiot" and "Stupid" guides. A relative of mine used to tease me for buying those books, saying he refused to buy a book that said he was an idiot.

I explained that he missed the point. The purpose of a good self-help book is to take you back to yourself and the beginning of your knowledge about something. It's not that any of us are idiots or stupid about anything. Essentially, we're all to some degree ignorant, innocent, or naïve about some aspect of our lives.

A baby struggles to breathe Day One and then gets that skill down pat. Then walking becomes the skill to master, then riding a bike. At some point the baby, now adult, learns to drive a car. In other words, life is a series of lessons to find ways to propel ourselves forward.

Again, the bottom line does end up being about not allowing yourself to be a victim even when others try to engage in victimizing behavior. That's why while almost all blacks may instinctively operate from the gut level of being survivors, strivers, or thrivers, ultimately, what we should all aim to be are drivers— drivers of our lives, our career paths, and our destinies. Whether you run a forklift or you run the financial division of a Fortune 500 company, you want to be the driving force behind how you got where you are, the nature of your experiences while you are there, and whether you want to continue to stay or move forward to something else.

The thing to remember is that all black employees deal with that 15 percent difference and it can be some comfort to know you're not alone. The key is how you choose to deal with it.

2

WHERE TO BE A BLACK EMPLOYEE IN WHITE AMERICA

Richard clerked for a law firm in a Southern city the summer between his second and third year of law school in the mid-1990s. The clerkship was for one of those huge firms that you see in the movies. For a law student, a summer clerkship is typically the ticket to get you a job when you graduate from law school.

Although Richard loved the money he was making that summer—more money than he knew people even could make in a week—he didn't like the fact that he was the only black summer clerk. But Richard chose to just be happy to be nappy, and to take it all in stride. There were black attorneys and other blacks employed in the firm, so he figured if he could just get the job in the end, well, it would all work out.

All summer long, Richard worked his butt off. He wrote tons of memos, researched for hours on end, and was generally known as a bright and friendly guy. In addition to doing the work, he also did a big part of the extras that were required—schmoozed with all the white people. He did the dinner parties and the canoe trip and the lunches and the barbecues. He even did the country-western party with a smile on his face.

Richard put the emphasis on the work. He knocked himself out paying attention to every little detail so that when the summer was over he could get the call offering him a job.

Fast forward to August when he got his end-of-the-summer review from one of the partners.

"Great work product." Check. "Outstanding work ethic." Check. "Overall, one of the best clerks this summer." Heading to a homerun. "There's just one little concern, however, Richard." Uh oh. "One of the partners who went on the firm-sponsored canoe trip we took was concerned about the fact that you made some remark about being the only black person in a hundred-mile radius of the town where the canoe trip was located."

Richard suddenly knew what the phrase "seeing red" meant. He had never had a truly violent impulse in his life, but if ever there were a time he felt like busting heads, it was at that moment. He sat there while the partner inquired about his ability to work with whites, report to whites, deal with whites. Richard couldn't believe that in the 1990s, he was dealing with this in an evaluation as if this were a legitimate issue.

As a black person in America, working for a living is pretty much the one thing in life you're going to do. Like brushing your teeth in the morning, it's not something that you can do once and expect it to cover you for the rest of your life. Working is something that you pretty much have to keep doing. Working presents a lifetime of decisions and choices.

The concept of choices does not just start with the first job, either. It used to be common for people, particularly blacks who had limited choices to begin with, to get a job when they graduated from high school or college and stay at the same job until they retired. With most black families, because slavery and Jim Crow are a part of our legacy, making a *good* decision about a job used to involve no more analysis than asking did it pay well and have benefits. If you came from one of the privileged, Talented Tenth type of families, then you might be pressured to join a profession such as law or medicine, or pushed to own a business. (Black intellectual W. E. B. DuBois coined the phrased "Talented Tenth" in the early 1900s to describe the top 10 percent of Negroes who should seck higher education, rather than the industrial training opportunities espoused by Booker T. Washington.)

Starting in the 1960s, with the advent of better (but not perfect) laws and expanding social consciousness, opportunities improved and so did the range of choices for black Americans.

Richard's example may not be typical of what happens to a black legal intern, but it does show that as the stakes go up, so does the range of choices, problems, and opportunities.

The last thing Richard expected in his end-of-the-summer evaluation was to have to defend himself against allegations that he noticed he was black. Richard, nevertheless, with more heat than he had ever shown during that long hot summer of working, asked the partner if he was interrogating the more than a dozen white clerks on their ability to get along with blacks and other ethnic groups. Richard asked if the other clerks' performances would be held hostage to their skill on dealing with black judges, black opposing counsel, black clients, or black witnesses.

Richard ended his evaluation telling the partner that if Big Southern Fried Law Firm wanted to hire blacks who could forget their race the second they got to work, then he wasn't someone they should hire. As his parting shot, Richard also stated that instead of questioning the lone black clerk about his ability to get along with whites because of one comment, maybe the firm ought to question why they felt it *fun* to take an annual firm-sponsored canoe trip three hours away to an area well known for the presence of the Ku Klux Klan.

In the end, Richard got the job offer, worked for the firm for a few years, and left when he figured out that his gut instincts about really being able to succeed in that firm were correct—that his skin color would make it harder to make that climb to partnership in the firm. He wanted to believe that the anonymous partner's obvious racism was an aberration. Instead, what Richard found out was that while the partner's blatant racism was an aberration, Richard was way too tall for the glass ceiling that mysteriously hovered over the heads of the black attorneys in this particular firm. So Richard made the most of this experience—after all, Big Southern Fried Law Firm looked impressive on his resume—and then he followed his gut and moved on. (Richard was a striver.)

Let's be clear—Richard was a success. He may have faced some discrimination, bigotry, and insensitivity, but he was a success. Richard got the education he wanted, he got the job he wanted, and, most important, he got to fulfill his dream of being a litigator. You see, that's the problem that a large number of whites don't get. They truly want to believe that racism and discrimination can be avoided by a black willing and able to do the "right" things. Like growing up on the wrong side of the tracks, they want to believe that race is merely a pesky hurdle to be jumped over with the right motivation.

Well, that's not true and I'm not going to say otherwise. Race is not an impediment, but it is a *reality* you work *through* on the road to achieving all the things you are going to achieve anyway. There aren't two groups of blacks who exist—those who have race touch their work experience and those who don't. All blacks experience it. Some are aware of it. Some are hyperaware of it. Some have major problems with it in the workplace. Some experience mild speed bumps in a glorious career.

Race is always a factor. Period. There is no thinking, breathing, functioning black employee who will tell you that race hasn't touched her experience if she's ever worked someplace where she was in the minority. It doesn't touch every aspect of work, but it touches enough of the overall experience to require you to empower yourself with the perspective and knowledge to make sure that your work life is as positive as you can make it. Know that when you do hit certain hurdles, you are not alone. Even if no white boss, coworker, friend, or stranger understands, I do and so do a lot of other blacks.

When it's all said and done, blacks working for whites encounter the same dilemmas, the same problems, the same concerns no matter what part of the country we live in, no matter how much or how little money we make, or how many laws, history, degrees, and support groups we have to protect us. We're still a potent—but small—part of the population who stand out loud and clear. With some exception, people have to figure out if you are Catholic, Republican, or vegetarian, but they usually don't have to figure out if you're black. Combined with the fact that blacks are the group most associated with the civil rights movement, where you find a black person in a mostly white work environment is where you find someone who didn't get in on a free pass. That's why when, for example, white Americans say that they don't "see" Colin Powell's race, we all know that's bullshit. They admire Powell so much because they know how many barriers he had to overcome, and this is why it is important for us to work smarter before we even begin working.

How you start is how you finish.

Learn from Our Legacy

Blacks have the most complex working history of any group in America. We don't have to travel too far up our ancestral line to find relatives who didn't work for pay—they worked to keep from being beaten or killed, they worked because they and their children (if they even got to keep them) were property, they worked because that was the norm and they weren't supposed to remember any other reality. This is our history. We did not try to get here by boat, by foot, or by sneaking through any way we could to make a better life for ourselves and our families—that is the history of others. We were brought here as property to help others build better lives for their own families. We were used like bricks, like horses, like river water to provide labor for the birth of a nation.

From Middle Passage to slavery, we move to the Fifteenth Amendment, to Jim Crow, and smack dab up to Title VII in 1964 making discrimination in the workplace unlawful. Basically, blacks did not have quite the same succession plan as other groups. Historians have argued that with all the roadblocks put in place, it wasn't truly until the Voting Rights Act of 1965 that blacks actually had the right to vote. Therefore, from a practical standpoint, blacks didn't really start having the benefits of full citizenship in society until the mid-1960s. This includes the workplace.

My point is not that other ethnic groups did not have it bad, or that nonblack individuals (including whites) don't have their share of issues in the workplace. It's just that in America, the history of blacks is unique, and whatever issues our mere presence brings up with whites, these kick into place immediately. For example, in some situations the 15 percent difference gets triggered when the recruiter who takes your application puts it at the bottom of the pile because she doesn't like black people. Therefore, with the exception of blacks who can pass for white (or at least nonblack), the majority of blacks do not have the option of waiting until after we prove ourselves to identify ourselves as black. It's like the old skit from the television show *In Living Color*: an overeager, overslick brother (performed by Tommy Davidson) always ends up having a conversation with someone that ends with him startling the person by pulling out his business card, abruptly sticking it in their face, and shouting "Bam!" That's what showing up at the job as a black person is like.

One of the things that I have repeatedly heard whites say is that blacks just need to get over slavery. It's in the past, man. Let it go, dude. They're right. Slavery is done. But the remnants of slavery continue to exist and proliferate. As black people who work, our legacy of being the descendants of bought goods still lingers. Right now, Johnnie Cochran is probably the single most well known living black attorney in this country. We loved Thurgood

Marshall and we've all heard of Clarence Thomas, but when any of us starts thinking about who we would want to represent us if we were ever on trial for murder, Johnnie immediately springs to mind.

Well, did you know that Cochran's great-grandfather was a slave? Think about that for a second. Only two generations stand between Johnnie Cochran and slavery. Take that a step further. There are no slaves without slave owners. Therefore, when Cochran is going toe-to-toe with opposing counsel, witnesses, prosecutors, and judges, many of them only have two generations that stand between them and being slave owners.

This is our legacy and we experience it every day. Less than one month before the start of 2003, Senate Majority Leader Trent Lott had to apologize for indirectly singing the praises of a segregated America. (He was later forced to resign as majority leader.) His view may not be the majority view, but it exists.

Blacks have a historical legacy of unfair treatment, but we can shape our individual legacies so that the collective goals we've achieved in this society move us forward as a people.

For example, I wrote about Johnnie Cochran's situation in terms of his historical legacy, but what you've got to admire about Cochran when you see him on television is that he clearly loves what he is doing. He gets a charge from being "Da Man." You can't tell me that—while I'm sure he took the O. J. Simpson trial and its aftermath very seriously—he didn't get a little kick from the fact that "If it don't fit, you must acquit" became a household phrase.

We all can't be Johnnie Cochran. But we all can aim for having work situations that empower us and make us feel that, while we may stand out, we still have infinitely more say in our work situations than our great-grandparents did.

Learn to Be a Driver

If you're just starting off in the workforce, ask yourself what you really want to do. If you're smack dab in the middle of the workforce, ask yourself do you want to keep doing this particular job or maintaining this career path, or do you want to do something else?

Because of our history and fear, black people tend to keep our range of choices very narrow. I know of many people who work where they work because their cousin told them a company was hiring, or because most of the people in the neighborhood work for a certain industry. In black families especially, you see that dynamic play out—you'll see a family that has four out of five children in the military, or where all the children grew up to be middle-class professionals.

My friends know that when they seek my counsel on whether they should leave a particular job, one of my common things to say is that they should never run from a job, they should only run to a better job. In other words, don't stay in miserable situations and then find yourself just having to get another job quickly to pay the bills. Figure out what you really want to do and then find a way to create that opportunity, so that the next job begins with joy and excitement.

Sometimes that great job may be something you find in the want ads or on an Internet job site. But you still need to figure out who you are and what you like before you start searching.

For a black person, the ultimate strategy as a driver is to seek out the people who are most happy with their jobs and figure out how to get there. Don't go by a title. Too many people (OK, too many black people, in my opinion) judge someone's happiness by what he earns instead of asking the person whether he derives joy from what he does. We also fail to take ownership of the fact that we can be the driving force behind finding joy in whatever job we do. Sometimes moving on to the next job is not the point or the goal. Sometimes it's finding the joy in the job you have.

However, if you identify a specific new job or career you desire, be a driver—make sure you figure out exactly what stands between you and getting what you want. Break it down into as many small steps as you can. I think it's a Chinese proverb that says the longest journey begins with the first and smallest step. Maybe it's just picking up the phone and getting information from the financial aid office at your local college. Maybe it's e-mailing the company you want to work for and asking them to send you the requirements for the job listing they posted on an Internet site. Part of being a successful black driver is looking inside yourself and discovering what you want, instead of constantly trying to look at what decisions every other black is making. So what if you're the first black to hold down a certain job. If you feel driven to do it, just assess the situation ahead of time and go for it.

The first step toward figuring out what you want to do for a living, if you haven't started yet or want to make a change, involves getting in touch with what makes you tick.

If you're 45 and thinking about a job change, that's a lot easier than when you're 18 and thinking about that first job. The beauty of the workforce is that you're allowed to change your mind even if the first job or the first 10 jobs aren't quite right for you. Your job is not who you are, but working is what you do and it should reflect who you are.

When I meet people in social settings I usually dread the part where they ask what I do for a living, because once they ask and I say that I'm a lawyer, they superimpose a whole set of assumptions on me about my personality, my hobbies, how I grew up, my interests. They even think they know what kind of car I must drive. (Of course, I'm embarrassed to say I sometimes do the same thing when I meet people and they tell me what they do for a living.)

The truth is that most of us stumble into our jobs, careers, or professions. I didn't start law school until I was 27 years old because I had never met a lawyer in my life until I was in my mid-20s and had always thought that people like me didn't become lawyers. I knew of only one other person in my family with a college degree and she was a teacher, something I knew I didn't want to do.

Even as a youngster, you collect plenty of information about jobs, even if it's just figuring out what you don't want to do. If your uncle is an army major who travels around the world and you love hearing about all the places he's visited, you've got a key piece of information about yourself and what you might want to do for a living. You might not necessarily want to be in the military because you don't like regimentation, but you want a job that takes you to a lot of places. Find other jobs that provide the same opportunity to travel.

Let's say you know you are a family-oriented person. Your favorite moments involve spending time with your family. That's the most important thing to you. Knowing something as simple as that can trigger a host of questions about what kind of employment you want to have. Do you just like spending time around your own family or do you like being around families in general? Do you like hanging around the children or the older folks? Do you like teaching your family how to do things, or do you like being the family cook? That's an example of how the process of asking yourself questions gets you to a good answer.

Exploring our maximum range of options is a skill we black Americans are still trying to teach ourselves.

One of the reasons I mentally divide blacks into the categories of survivor, striver, and thriver is because those three groups use different considerations to make decisions about where they are going to work or how they are going to make money.

Think about the range of different ways there are to make money, once you eliminate those that are illegal. Some people start their own companies and businesses. Then there are the people who get degrees and enter professions. Whether professional or not, there are jobs in private industry and there are government jobs. Within private industry, there are small companies, medium-sized ones, and huge corporations. In addition, there are people who enlist in the military or the Peace Corps, and folks who hone their skills and talents to be entertainers or athletes. Some people find jobs that allow them to serve God, such as ministers, priests, nuns.

This book couldn't begin to tell you enough about any of those jobs to help you make an informed decision about which one is best for you. What I am is a believer in the ability to always make a change when it is in your best interest to make the change intelligently.

The book *What Color Is Your Parachute?* says that most people change jobs several times in their lifetimes. Good!!!!! As people grow, their aspirations change, just like their clothing styles or tastes in food. That's why you might have wanted to be a basketball player when you were 10 years old but when you're 18 and about to graduate from high school, you don't really see yourself being gifted enough to have any job that involves handling a ball for pay, especially when you get more of a kick from playing with computers.

Somewhere along the line, however, people (blacks included) bought into the false belief that by 18 or 21, you were competent to make a career choice for the rest of your life. Your driver's license is brand-new, you just got the right to leave your mama's house without having to check in after midnight, and legally drinking in public still doesn't feel quite right, but you're supposed to pick work that you know you're going to want to do in 10, 20, or 40 years? Yeah, right.

The following are two examples of what I'm talking about— one person who doesn't sit firmly in the driver's seat, and one who's not only firmly in the driver's seat but has a seatbelt fastened and a road map.

First there's a person named Georgia who kept switching between being a survivor, a striver, and a thriver because she did not get a good hold on what exactly she wanted to do before entering the job market.

Georgia, an educated professional black woman in her early 30s, usually cycles through being a survivor, striver, and thriver in a job, all in about a year's time before she moves on to another job when things don't work out. Extremely competent and with impressive credentials, Georgia gets a job and starts off as a striver, trying to beat a path of success to a higher position within her organization almost as soon as she arrives. She quickly realizes that the path to success won't be quite that direct. Once she realizes this, she becomes a thriver. Her hairdos start getting more experimental, she becomes more outspoken about controversial views, and she begins expressing a more daredevil, "what-the-f—k" attitude. The good thing is that Georgia always manages to maintain a high level of quality in her work, no matter what stage she spirals in. However, at some point, either her coworkers, her boss, or her own fear factors start kicking in and setting off alarms. So then Georgia smooth moves to a survivor mentality either because she's worried about keeping her job or because she gets bored enough to start looking for a new job anyplace else.

That particular cycle works for my friend Georgia, or at least until recently it has. It's worked in the past because she is incredibly gifted at each job she does, she always leaves on a good note and on her own terms, and she always lands on her feet finding another job before she quits the one she's unhappy with.

However, what my friend is beginning to realize is that being aware of her agenda before she starts a new job is key to not defaulting from a striver into either of these other mentalities. Georgia realizes that she is getting too old not to have longevity at one job in a career that respects staying power. Since at essence Georgia is a striver, being a survivor and a thriver are default mechanisms for her, so she needs to figure out what she ultimately wants to do and find a job that gets her there from Day One.

In Georgia's defense, it wasn't exactly that she hadn't thought about what she wanted to do. She had thought about it. However, like a lot of first-generation college students in black families, she didn't have any role models for how to figure out a life path. She picked philosophy as her undergraduate major, but then felt she needed to go to law school to get a practical job. However, once she got the practical graduate degree, she spent the next few years job-hopping in frustration.

The second example—of someone who has undertaken his career as a driver and been successful—is a brother I know who scoped out his life goals and career plan from the beginning.

Tony came from a background where he wasn't the first generation to go to college, own a business, or earn middle-class pocket change. Since Tony knew he wanted to be in politics by 30 years of age, when it came time to pick one of two companies who offered him a job right out of college, he picked the company that had the better track record where blacks were concerned. Ironically, the company he rejected had more blacks working there, but those blacks encountered more obstacles and were more crowded around the bottom of the ladder. Tony was the prototype of a black striver and he wasn't about to slow his path to the pinnacle. Tony ran for city council at the age of 30, but missed winning the election by a hair because he ran against an established white incumbent. There's no doubt in my mind that with the name recognition he acquired, the community support he built, and the taste of victory in his well-honed taste buds, Tony will only be off by a couple of years in meeting his goal of holding political office by the age of 30.

My point isn't that Tony is Mr. Golden Black Man who made perfect decisions and encountered no roadblocks in his career path. It certainly is not to imply that his path didn't come littered with those same 15 percent issues that Georgia's did. It's just that his plan was so fixed in his mind and his path was so sure, those 15 percent issues were obstacles he got around differently. He wasn't luckier than Georgia or smarter than Georgia. His people just had a head start on Georgia's people in whittling out better opportunities and success strategies that were then passed down to Tony.

Figure Out Where and How to Work

I can't tell you how to pick a job or a career. That's part of the 85 percent piece everyone has to figure out for him- or herself. Ways to help you figure out where to work and how to work include:

- Going through the classified job section of the Sunday newspaper from A to Z and circling all the jobs that interest you, regardless of your qualifications
- Talking to people about what they do and do not like about their jobs
- Going to the library and checking out the career section
- Seeking out a headhunter or a job coach
- Exposing yourself to as many different kinds of jobs and careers as you can to see what fits

My personal philosophy, as I've gotten older and a little further along in my own career, is that I don't look for jobs, I create opportunities. Rather than looking for a job and then figuring out whether I want to do that particular set of duties, I find I'm happier when I figure out what I like to do and find the opportunity that pays me to do it. I wish I had approached jobs that way when I started my career because it would have saved me at least a couple of wrong turns. Of course, the truth is, the wrong turns taught me lessons each time that helped with the next round of decisions.

Even a black person right out of high school or college can create opportunities if she does her homework and thinks carefully about what she wants. What's your intention? Are you looking for a job or a career? A trade or a profession? If you don't know, you may end up someplace that you don't like. It's like the old joke about the person who got lost while driving but made good time getting to the place where he ended up.

When it comes to working, you should never stop asking yourself these questions unless you're deliriously happy with what you're doing. In fact, the longer you ask these questions without paying attention to your own answers, the longer it takes you to find the right vocation for yourself.

A friend of mine is a beautiful and brilliant sister in her early 30s who wants to be a doctor. She has wanted to be a doctor for years and keeps going back to college for classes and the occasional degree or certification. She also finds jobs in the health care industry, which is the equivalent of having her nose pressed against a store window. I once asked her why, since she's single and has no kids, she just didn't go to medical school full-time. Her answer was that by the time she took the necessary courses, studied, took the MCAT, graduated from medical school, and did a residency or two, she would be in her 40s. Of course, I made the classic response by asking her if she wasn't going to be in her 40s in seven or eight years anyway. One day I think she'll go to medical school and kick herself for not starting earlier. Or she won't and will spend her 40s and the years after that regretting not having done so.

Another friend of mine waited until her mid-40s to get a college degree. She did this after raising a family, divorcing a husband, and working more than a dozen years at a utility company. After she achieved this first degree, she got the itch and kept going to school until she ended up with a Ph.D., and now, in her 60s, is a college professor. She focused on a dream and her intention, asked the right questions of herself and others, did the research, dug for the resources, and ended up doing what she wanted to do. So what if she started this career in her 50s—she was happy every step of the way. Did she ever and does she still face discrimination in a world that kneels at the altars of youth, fair skin, and masculinity? Yes, of course. But because she knew what she wanted, she surrounded herself with the energy, the information, and the people who helped her navigate those waters.

Not everyone aims to be a doctor or a college professor. It may be that your goal is to get an earlier work shift so that you can spend more time with your kids, or maybe you want to be a disc jockey at a radio station rather than just listening to the radio while you input computer data.

The point is that picking a job or a career is not something you do once in your life. Examining whether you are happy and fulfilled in what you do for pay is an ongoing journey with no real destination until you stop working.

Again, the point is not that you get around the 15 percent issues of being black in the workplace by picking the "right" job or career; rather, it is that you withstand those 15 percent issues better when you pick the job or career that is right for you.

3

AIN'T TOO PROUD TO BEG

How Blacks Get Through
the Door in the First Place

■

Maggie was the first person in her family to go to college. She was raised by a single mother, and Maggie had three children herself by the age of 18.

By the time Maggie graduated from college, she was a striver pure and simple, ready to take on the world and make a better life for herself and her children. When she was about to graduate from engineering school, she was, therefore, quite proud of her accomplishments. She felt like it reflected on her character and tenacity, that she could graduate from college while raising children.

In the section of her resume dealing with accomplishments, Maggie always listed raising her children, including

each of their ages. Maggie wondered why she had trouble
getting called back for job interviews.

Maggie had every right to be proud of her achievements as a
black woman raising three children with little help from either
the fathers of the children or her own family, but we live in a
world of stereotypes. In addition to listing her three children
and their ages, Maggie also gave a detailed list of the black asso-
ciations she belonged to, such as the college chapter of the
NAACP and the black Engineering Students. Therefore, anyone simply skimming her resume saw the neon light flashing
"single black mother up ahead." Even for a thriver, a black
employee who lives life according to his or her own rhythm,
that's too much information before you get to the interview
stage.

Is the point that Maggie was supposed to hide the fact that
she had children? No, because the information itself was not the
issue. What Maggie needed to do was keep in mind the 15 percent factor. When applying for a job, *any* mother, regardless of
race, must be particularly wise regarding the appropriate time to
reveal this information. A black single mother needs to be particularly sensitive. The bottom line is that there is a stereotype
that black women and girls are more promiscuous than white
women and girls. Therefore, Maggie should have anticipated that,
employment laws aside, future employers might jump to the conclusion that she had some wild streak as a teenager that she still
might have as an adult. Leaving the information about her children off her resume will buy Maggie the necessary window of

time to impress a potential employer with her qualifications *before* giving them a chance to jump to conclusions just from looking at a piece of paper.

Jeremy is a journalist who applies for jobs in his profession carefully, strategically, and with audacity. Since college he was clear about what he wanted to do with his career and his life. His goals included working at his hometown newspaper, then working at well-respected national newspapers, and ultimately winning prestigious awards for his writing. By the age of 40, Jeremy had done all three because he wasn't merely responding to life, but had made himself the driving force deciding the path of his professional life.

One of the ways he did this was by learning from his mistakes—or figuring out why his actions didn't always match the results he wanted. For example, early on in his career when he applied for jobs he didn't get, sometimes he would politely ask an interviewer what he could have done differently to get the job. He adjusted (never falsified) his resume when necessary, changed his interview style when suggested, and used his results (plus further investigation) as his learning tools. For example, when one potential employer told Jeremy that he needed more hard news experience to supplement his extensive feature writing experience, he made a point of asking for more opportunities to cover breaking news stories at the newspaper where he worked (without telling his current employer why) before applying for other jobs.

In terms of applying for a job, Jeremy is clearly a driver. While instinctively a striver, Jeremy becomes a driver when he takes his strategy one step further. While the striver operates from ambition, a driver operates from the best instincts of the survivor (such as to not do anything that endangers getting or keeping a job) and thriver (such as operating with his own flair), while keeping the liabilities of those modes of transportation to a minimum.

Jeremy recognized that, when it comes to getting a job, he pays more attention to the 85 percent issues—how he as a potential employee is well suited for a particular job—in order to eliminate any doubts that this potential employee, who happens to be black, can do the job and do it well.

How can Maggie be a driver? By realizing that, ultimately, no employer really cares whether you have a kid or not as long as having children won't interfere with how you perform your job. Therefore, Maggie should highlight the qualifications that make her stand out as the best person for a particular job. This needs to be her driving motivation. That's where research, like what Jeremy did, comes in handy. If you've done basic research to figure out what skills you need to excel in a particular corporate culture and what the job qualifications are for a particular position, then it's not a stretch to list the qualifications you have that make you stand out as a strong candidate for the job.

This chapter deals with one of the first ways that the 15 percent issue can rear its head for a black employee. After all, if race is going to be an issue in the workplace, getting through the door is probably the first place that will come up. For example, a study in 2002 conducted by two professors from the Massachusetts Institute of Technology and the University of Chicago Graduate School of Business found that resumes with black-sounding names got half as many responses from employers as resumes from those with white-sounding names.

What Am I Looking for, Anyway?

The question is, what information is a black person supposed to be fishing for anyway when figuring out how to get through the door? A black person who is a survivor will be the type of person who needs the least amount of information. Ultimately, his work experience is not going to be affected one way or the other. As long as there is not a huge discrepancy between what he makes and what others doing the same job make, he will be fine with the money issue. Survivors care somewhat if other blacks work with them, but it usually will not be a deal breaker.

Strivers, on the other hand, will need to know a lot of—pardon the pun—black and white information. How many blacks work at the company? What positions do they hold? What prompted the blacks who left to leave? Has a black person ever done the job I'm hired to do? Has a black ever been promoted to the types of jobs I might want to do?

Thrivers have the toughest research job of all, because their research will center on style and culture and the intangible things that can determine whether they despise going to work. Is it corporate clingy or laid-back smooth? Is the place weighed down with rules and regulations? Will I get fired for expressing opinions? Am I going to stand out to the point where it will interfere with me doing my job? A thriver finds this out by asking about the personalities of the black folks and the white folks. More important, the thriver finds this out by figuring out what blacks work there and why. A thriver may or may not be what the employer thinks of as a troublemaker, but you certainly don't want to walk into an environment where you will almost certainly be labeled one because of how you compare to everyone else.

On the surface, it's all an 85 percent issue. Employers advertise for jobs, "equal employment opportunity" signs hang out all over, and affirmative action programs still exist. It doesn't seem like it should be that complicated. However, statistics show that the two areas of life where blacks probably experience the most discrimination are in employment and housing. According to a review of the latest U.S. census data, a black household made an average of $649 for every $1,000 that a white household made. There aren't any statistics that show how many blacks are turned away at the hiring stage because of race, since no employer is going to admit to that reason in a survey and every employee who believes race is the reason doesn't necessarily report it. But with such a huge disparity between white and black incomes, it's clear that more higher paying jobs are going to whites than to blacks.

Going After the Job You Want

You should never apply for a job unless you know you want the job. A black person has to go through an extra analysis of how race may play a role in situations that involve a predominantly white environment. Taking the time to do this extra analysis thoroughly is never more important than before you interview to get a job. Whether you are a survivor, a striver, or a thriver makes no difference if you don't get the job in the first place, or if you get the wrong job.

Usually, getting a job with anyone, particularly white folks, starts off with that first piece of paper. For some blacks, that first piece of paper is a job application, for others it's a resume. Sometimes it's both. Sometimes it's just seeing an ad in the newspaper and showing up.

But at some point, you are expected to put in print things about yourself that reveal who you are and tell your employer who you're going to be as a worker. So be sure you want the job—any job—before you go through all the trouble to do your extra evaluation and research.

Research, Research, Research

One of the first things that a black person needs to do before applying for a job is research the company. It's amazing to me how few people do that. As far as I'm concerned, it's an essential step to decide if you even want to work for a given company. Even if your research comes up empty or you get wrong information, it's far better than the alternative—trying to drive at night with your headlights off.

For blacks, getting the lowdown on a company is critical information. You've got to know how many other blacks work there, how many of them are managers or supervisors, and what the story is about the blacks who no longer work there.

Being a former newspaper reporter, I'm usually the go-to guy for my friends when they want advice on how to find out this kind of information. My standard reply is start with common sense and move on from there.

The great little secret about being black is that what whites suspect is true—we truly do all know each other. OK, maybe we don't directly, but there usually is an indirect line from you to a black person who knows something about Corporation X. Ask your mama. Ask your cousin Peaches. Ask another black person in the industry. Pick the brains of your white friends. If you choose your white friends with as much care as I do, then they will be almost as likely as most blacks to give you the lowdown on what the environment is really like. When you don't take advantage of the six degrees of separation that exist between you and your next job, you're playing Negro Roulette if you take the job anyway.

> Malika went to work for a marketing company. She had heard good things about the company in general, so she focused on the overall reputation of the organization within the industry and figured any other issues wouldn't be important. Well, she got the job and, even though it was the year 2000, she found herself the first black ever hired by the company and the only woman to be hired in a management position. That by itself would not have been a problem but for the fact that nobody in the company but the pseudoliberal who hired Malika was particularly interested in having a black woman working there, especially a black woman who made more money than just about everyone else in the company.

With just a little research and attention to the red flags, Malika might have saved herself the trouble of being an experiment that failed in a company that drained her spirit, zapped her confidence, and converted her from being a thriver to a survivor when she got her next job. Malika endured constant exclusion from lunch and other social activities (which furthered her political isolation within the company), repeated criticism about her lack of experience in a certain area of marketing (which she told them up front that she didn't have), and numerous comments about her salary and "how well" she was being paid compared to others.

Again, a good decision hinges on good research, and good research depends on knowing what you want before you have to make a decision. It's imperative that you choose job situations that put you where you want to be, based on your individual goals. Identifying those goals first will help make your research more directed and efficient.

Job Applications and Resumes

People who apply for jobs by filling out job applications, in some ways, have it easy. The person taking your application can see that you are black. You won't have the initial problem of an interviewer being caught off guard, in the event that your being black is going to catch someone by surprise when the time comes to interview. Although the person who collects the applications may not be the person who actually interviews, I always assume that your race gets passed along if it's not the majority. It's sort of like when you read a novel and the writer never mentions when the character is white but always makes a point of mentioning if the person is Black or Hispanic or Asian.

Resumes pose a trickier problem. Asking yourself important questions as you create your resume can't be avoided. Should I or shouldn't I put something down that indicates I'm black? Or should I play the *Guess Who's Coming to Dinner* surprise move and let them find out when I show up?

Again, how you start is how you finish. That's why sitting down and asking yourself what your mode of operation is will answer that question for you.

Some people, for example, want prospective employers to know up front that they are black so that a problem can be knocked out early. That has always been my personal philosophy, but even that may not be a clear-cut decision.

Are you essentially a survivor? Do you just want a job where you put in your time, collect your paycheck, and ease on down that road to retirement, or at least to steady paychecks until a better gig comes along? Then leave off all references to being black. Don't mention groups or organizations that have the word *black* in the title. That gets you two things. One, if they don't know you're black before you come in for the interview, many white employers will either not care that you are black or will be pleasantly surprised that you didn't broadcast it before the interview. Two, for the segment of employers who are supersensitive about race issues, an employer will be too focused on the reasons why she should hire you if she likes your resume than on worrying about the ways you may or may not fit in the organization once you get hired. Your personal employment goals will dictate how you react.

A striver wants to get through the door to get ahead. Therefore, a striver will be more concerned with the total package than whether or not he makes too many references to his race. The striver's resume will wave flags like "Professional Society of Black Engineers," "Black Secretaries of America," "Human Resources Black America." That's not a bad idea if done with a light hand. It portrays the applicant as being serious about his or her career without necessarily coming off as militant.

Now the thriver just ain't going to care. If he or she is the media spokesperson for the hometown chapter of the Black Panthers, that's going to have a high spot on her resume. The thriver will not be ashamed to tell you in bold letters on her resume that she was one of the founding chapter members of the All Black Symphony in her hometown. No accomplishment is off-limits for a thriver. Accomplishments, awards, and accolades that relate directly to black people are exactly what the thriver will highlight, if that is important to her.

The point is not that thrivers are going to be the biggest pro-black folks in the workplace. It's just that white people will think they will be. (On a personal note: I've never understood why most whites confuse exuberance or loudness or even passion with militancy. Many a time I've been the person that my white supervisors just knew, to paraphrase Michael Jackson, wanted to be starting sumthin', but a good two-thirds of the time, it was my nice, quiet, low-to-the-ground brother or sister who stood ready to riot and storm the gates when a problem arose.)

Guess Who's Coming to the Interview

One thing to remember as a black person trying to get that foot through the door, whether you're right out of school or whether you're working on your tenth job since the 1970s, is that who you are on paper is *not* necessarily who they are going to get as an employee.

You're trying to get a job, not bare your soul. Keeping anything other than need-to-know information off a resume or job application is not lying. (Warning: Never, ever, never lie on a resume. As a reporter, I've seen careers ruined with a lie, and as an attorney, I've seen lawsuits crumble over one lie.)

Beth provides a fine example of a resume that just screamed blond-haired, blue-eyed preppie: Ivy League school, cultured last name, corporate specializations, and classy hobbies and memberships, including a membership in the National Bar Association.

Oops. The NBA (also known as the *other* NBA), also known as "the black lawyers group." Well, what you see is what you get.

More than once, Beth has seen the look on the faces of interviewers change to blatant surprise when the porcelain pale maiden they expected turned out to be a dark shade of mahogany. Some jobs she didn't get. Some she did. But Beth's interviewers almost always got a surprise.

Affirmative Action or Acting

In the United States, one of the most interesting phenomena to me is that people think blacks are getting jobs left and right because of affirmative action. You know who I hear that from the most? Whites who didn't get jobs they wanted. Even if they don't know the race of the person who got the job, they'll swear on their own personal bible that they didn't get the job because of affirmative action.

What black folks know is that if affirmative action even crosses the mind of someone who is hiring us, that's not a good thing, because it means we will be held up to some artificial black standard we'll never live up to. For years, I've called it the "Super Nig" mentality. The Super Nig is supposed to do an A-plus job at all times, make no mistakes, and have hobbies and interests that make them fit in with all the white folks so that the company can pat itself on the back for finding such an "articulate" and "extraordinary" black hire. When ordinary black folks can't live up to the artificial perfection expected of Super Nig, that affirmative-action thinking employer feels justified in raising the standards even higher for the next black hire. My point isn't that every employer or supervisor harbors this mentality, but it is more prevalent than whites want to admit. It is the tendency to view the imperfections of black employees with a little more harshness in situations where the black employee is one of very few blacks in the workplace. Part of that comes from the fact that many whites are only used to dealing with blacks in forced environments—school and work—so stereotypes, usually dealing with work ethic or intelligence, do get passed on. Pretty much all black people are fighting a stereotype unless they work in the type of job where many blacks have come before them.

Frank was a white reporter I used to work with, who got passed over for about four different beat assignments in the two years I worked with him. Every time he didn't get the request, he would loudly say (in a room filled with black and Hispanic reporters) about how affirmative action was the reason he couldn't get ahead.

I really wanted to be the one to tell him how it was the original affirmative action—for white males—that got his incompetent ass hired in the first place and kept him from being fired in the second place, but I never wanted to put myself on the line by saying it.

In all the hundreds of employment cases I've been involved with as an attorney, I've never heard an employer use affirmative action or quotas as the reason for hiring a particular person of color, as opposed to having a general affirmative action plan. Actually, it tends to be the opposite. When white employers want to fire a black person (or member of another ethnic group), fear

of being accused of discrimination is what keeps them from firing the person sooner rather than later, even when it is a pretty
clear-cut case. An example is when a company let a black male
manager stay on for an indefinite period of time, even after the
company had received reliable written statements from his female
subordinates accusing him of sexual harassment. The company
was more afraid of a race discrimination claim from the black
manager than of the sexual harassment claims from the female
employees. Believe it or not, that hesitancy happens more than
black folks think.

Ultimately, getting caught up in a company's affirmative
action plan (or lack of one) doesn't do the average black person
any good. Some of the best, fairest companies to work for don't
have a formal plan at all, while some of the most racist, bigoted
companies will occasionally pay an advertising company to tout
them as the place to be if you're a person of color. That is why
cultivating good instincts is one of the most valuable tools any
person, but particularly a black person, can cultivate in the job-
hunting game. You have to fine-tune your ability to gauge
whether someone in the interviewing process doesn't care for you
regardless of your race, or whether the company or the department has general problems with hiring blacks. How do you cultivate those instincts? By listening carefully, taking good mental
notes, paying attention to your physical reactions, and then evaluating the outcome.

Lawful Questioning Only, Please

Under the law there are certain kinds of questions that a potential employer cannot ask you, but just because employers can't
ask the questions does not mean that they can't read between the

lines and blow you off anyway. Since getting the job is your goal, however, it may be in your best interest to address the underlying concern that even an unlawful question asks.

For example, a potential employer can usually ask you about criminal convictions relating to traffic violations and, in general, can ask you about criminal problems that relate directly to the job you are applying for. For example, if you're applying for a job to be a long-haul driver, your new boss has the right to know about those five speeding tickets you've received in the past seven years, because there is a direct correlation between your illegal speeding and what the potential employer is hiring you to do. Employers have legal liability for the employees they hire, so they have the right and the duty to ask. Similarly, if you apply for a job as a bookkeeper, your potential boss can ask you if you have any criminal convictions relating to whether you will have a tendency to poach money if hired. Again, the company has a duty to ask because they can get sued for negligent hiring otherwise.

Employers are not supposed to ask job applicants about arrests, however. The U.S. Department of Labor has recognized that asking about arrests is a loaded and particularly discriminatory question since one, an arrest is no indication of guilt, and two, minorities have historically suffered (and still suffer) more arrests than whites.

Credit is another tough one. Unless there is a business necessity (such as in any job in a bank that involves the handling of other people's money), the U.S. Department of Labor has determined that, in general, potential employees should not be asked about their credit records because those records tend to have an adverse effect on minorities. You need to read carefully any general waivers you sign when you apply for a job, however, because you may be signing a release that allows an employer to get a copy of your credit report. (The issue of credit is a book-length subject, but know that, traditionally, blacks have less money and worse credit than whites for reasons ranging from access to education to racism. Therefore, working to achieve and maintain good credit might end up being as important a factor in getting a job as in getting a new car.)

Kevin is a black man with a master's degree who lived overseas as a business consultant. He wanted to come back to America to be closer to his family. Actually, he didn't want to be too close to his Indiana-based family, but close enough in case of an emergency; therefore he applied for the perfect job in Atlanta. In his interview, Kevin signed a waiver allowing the company, a national corporation, to look at his credit report, his criminal records, any open civil records (such as being a party in a lawsuit), and basically everything else that could be uncovered about him with nothing more than a Social Security number. On the condition that everything from the background check turned out fine, the Atlanta company made a conditional job offer to Kevin. Kevin was confident that everything would work out just fine so he quit his current job, packed his bags, and found an apartment in Atlanta. While visiting his family in Indiana, waiting to start his new life, Kevin received word from the Atlanta firm that the job offer was rescinded based on a troubling credit report.

That's the nature of the at-will employment thing. (*At-will employment* means you can quit without giving a reason and, with the exception of illegal discrimination, a company can fire you without a reason.) Kevin had no employment contract, the company made sure the offer was conditional to cover themselves, and Kevin had given the company written permission to do this investigation.

Unfair? Maybe. Unlawful? Not necessarily.

Kevin could have avoided this circumstance by not quitting the job he had until the background check was officially over and a firm offer made by the new job, but what he went through is an important lesson to learn whether you're a survivor, striver, or thriver.

First, don't be a sitting duck. Before you start job searching, do your research to see if you're in an industry that requires background checks. If you are, or if you suspect there may be a problem with your credit, your criminal background, or an outstanding lawsuit against you, attempt to resolve the problems before you start job hunting.

Alternatively, you can prepare a preemptive strike. If you are being asked to sign a waiver for purposes of a background check, you might want to offer up anything that scars you as a potential problem before you actually sign the paper. Sometimes the very act of revealing it yourself, and explaining your own concern about the impression it makes, may be enough to keep the information from being a problem with the employer.

The problem with a preemptive strike is that you might alert a potential employer to an issue that they might never red flag independently. Truth is, just because a company says they will do a background check doesn't mean they really will, or that they'll closely examine what they find. The key thing is to anticipate the potential problem in your background and be prepared with a contextual explanation about how the situation arose. For example, you were going through a divorce at the time your credit went sour or the DUI came the night of your baby sister's college graduation. Don't lie, just be prepared to do damage control. Most important, when the new employer says the job is conditional, or in any way implies the background check is still ongoing, *don't* make a move—literally or figuratively—until you have an actual offer.

> A woman named Olivia, who had a handful of cute kids, applied for a job as a paralegal. Olivia mentioned her children during the interview. Olivia got the job. The main attorney responsible for hiring Olivia patted herself on the back to several people about how she gave a poor, black, single mother a job. She was proud of her contribution to society. The only little problem was that Olivia had a husband. A great, hardworking, upstanding brother. That kind of blew the main old girl's attempt to help the black race uplift itself. Suddenly, Olivia was Public Enemy Number One—couldn't get a break from the partner who previously was her biggest supporter. Stereotypes. A bitch, ain't they?

So, what's the solution? Maggie mentions her kids on her resume and can't get a break, Olivia mentions her kids in the interview and gets too much of one. Children are really beside the point. Maggie's problem was one she could have anticipated and warded off with artful timing. Olivia just had the misfortune of applying for a job with an interviewer who had issues. Sometimes, the employer can reveal those problematic issues as early as the interview stage.

■

Interviewing is the first dance you have with your potential employers. They can ask good questions, which allow you to convince them to offer you a job, or they can ask really bad questions that leave you in a trick bag. Some of those bad questions can be downright unlawful. Knowing the difference will help you navigate these potentially treacherous waters.

What happens when someone is asked an unlawful question during a job interview? For example, a woman who is asked if her husband will mind the long hours she has to work (assuming that the candidate has volunteered that she is married, because asking is typically unlawful) might choose to answer the question because she is burning to have that particular job. But, because it is unlawful, there are other ways she could handle it. She could directly confront the person who asked the question by pointing out that it is unlawful. But then she risks being perceived as defensive. However, if she were indifferent about getting the job, she could report it to her state or federal Equal Opportunity office.

The key thing to remember when interviewing is to keep your eye on the prize; in other words, focus on getting the job offer in the first place before you decide whether you want to accept it. If you're concerned with getting the job, it may not be the best strategy for you to be thinking simultaneously about whether a question is illegal or not. Be more concerned with what the questions you are being asked reveal to you about your fit with that job or that supervisor. Take note of what topics the interviewer appears to keep getting back to. Is he concerned about your extracurricular activities? Does he keep dancing around the topic of any possible family distractions? Does he seem to focus on aspects of the job that you don't have a lot of experience and/or interest in? Take the questions asked as information to file away for your own decision-making process to help you determine your fit into that company or office.

Another preemployment matter that can come up is job testing. Some careers and jobs require them. How do you handle them? That's a tough one, because a variety of tests exists. There are civil service exams, which you can study for. Then there are personality tests, which you can't study for because, well, they're supposed to reveal your personality.

Many standardized tests have been criticized for reflecting cultural bias. They're written by white people to hire white people. No universal tips exist for taking any of them except for the obvious, such as asking if there are study aids or classes and taking advantage of them. If you know that a test will be given, take the time to study for it. If you really want the job, it won't feel like a burden. Give yourself every opportunity to succeed and don't assume cultural bias. Remember that unless your prospective employer is singling you out to take a test, which you could only learn about by talking to others applying for the same job, just chalk that up to the price that everyone has to pay to get the job. As long as you are confident that everyone applying for the job takes the test, you know you have an 85 percent issue.

How will you know when the 15 percent factor kicks in? You really won't unless you didn't get the job based on the tests and you challenge the company.

Adjusting Your Strategy in Hard Economic Times

When the economy goes belly up, sometimes the trick is getting any job. And since blacks historically have twice the unemployment rate as whites in this country, hard economic times hit blacks doubly hard. Therefore, sometimes the dream job just has to wait. When circumstances place you in the position of needing to find a job quickly for survival's sake, how do you speed up the process? First, you have to investigate who is hiring. In part, you can look through the Sunday want ads to see who is hiring. If you're a professional, then you can ask colleagues to recommend a good headhunter. (A headhunter puts professionals looking for jobs in touch with employers.) Employment agencies do the same thing for job hunters. Sometimes a middleman can speed up the process of looking for a job, but it will rarely be a good idea to rely on just that avenue. Working for a temporary agency might also be another way to get an idea of what's going on in a particular industry—a chance to get your feet wet before you dive in.

As far as taking advantage of affirmative action—good luck. Companies usually don't advertise or publicize their affirmative action goals for purposes of hiring. You might hear about them by word of mouth, but the signs advertising "Equal Opportunity Employer" are the equivalent of a restaurant with a sign that says "Our Kitchen Passes the Health Code."

Unfortunately, figuring out whether you've been discriminated against at the hiring stage is difficult to determine because you don't have a personal track record with the company. In other words, a rejection is usually a terse, impersonal communication without an explanation.

Some Final Thoughts

If you're experiencing an ongoing problem with finding a job, the problem may be with your job references. One of the ways you can test what your former employers are saying about you is to convince an intelligent-sounding and trustworthy friend to pretend to be a potential employer who is checking references you listed on your resume or application. It may be that you've been blackballed by getting negative references from one or more of your former employers. While some states allow you to sue your former employer for giving a bad reference (which is why many employers give out almost no real information anymore when another company calls for a reference), your real priority needs to be getting a job ASAP. A bad reference or just a plain uninspiring one will require you to think about providing another name or obtaining a written letter of reference that overflows with accolades.

Also, in job hunting, following up with a thank-you note to the interviewers is always a good idea. I've actually heard interviewers say the person who sent the note got the edge over all the other equally qualified candidates who didn't. That is an example of having the 15 percent difference work in your favor. To the extent that an interviewer has bad impressions about blacks or just indifferent ones, showing politeness and courtesy will make you stand out in a positive way that might help counteract a stereotype.

How you start is how you finish. So, in clarifying your intention before you begin job hunting, you have a much better likelihood of getting the job or career in the industry you want.

4

TALKING GOOD AND WELL

■

Martin had worked at his job as a manager of a Dallas department store for six months. He received his MBA from the
same black university where he'd received his undergraduate degree, which means he had minimal experience being
around whites before this job.

He thought things were going well, but he wasn't quite
sure. Martin figured that now, after being there for half a year,
it was time to get some feedback from his boss, Jack. "So,
Jack, I'm thinking of buying a brand-new car and before I do
that, I was curious about what you thought of my work
performance." Jack heartily responded, talking about the
joy and excitement of buying a brand-new car. He encour-
aged Martin to run out and buy one. However, Jack did not
address the question about Martin's work performance. Martin assumed, however, that Jack was saying that he was

doing a good job and that he had enough job security to make a major purchase. After all, Martin reasoned, he wouldn't put someone in that situation.

Based on his conversation with Jack, Martin got his first new car that weekend, complete with his first car payment. Two weeks later, Jack gave Martin his evaluation and his two weeks' notice, stating that his job was terminated due to extensive performance problems that dated back to when Martin first started.

Effective communication is probably one of the most important skills for success in the workplace. That's one of those 85 percent issues, relevant to every employee, since everyone needs good communication skills to get along and get ahead.

For a black employee, however, good communication is critical. When it is not done in a style compatible with the place a person works, an employee can easily find him- or herself dealing with that 15 percent difference.

What does it mean to communicate well? It is communication that gets your point across to the listener exactly as you intend; that is, that the listener gets the point you are trying to make. Good communication covers both the written and the spoken word. Good communication also includes the subtle body language that either deflects or reinforces what you are trying to say.

In the example above, Martin may have thought he was communicating well, but he wasn't. If he had been paying attention to Jack all along, he would have observed that Jack was not a very direct person. He would have observed this from the way Jack dealt with other people, saying one thing to people in Martin's presence, and then saying what he really thought after the people left. It was not that Jack was dishonest; Jack was just less than direct.

One of the biggest culture shocks for blacks who do not have any significant contact with whites until they are grown or nearly grown is dealing with the white tendency to be less direct than what most of us are used to.

Martin's boss, Jack, knew that he was about to terminate Martin when Martin asked about buying the car, because the performance problems dated back to the time when Martin started. Jack was being polite. In terms of communication, whites are more indirect and more concerned about politeness, unless the words are cloaked in authority. The direct thing for Jack to have said was, "Martin, if I were you, I wouldn't buy a scooter until after you've had your evaluation."

Let's face it, with a few Cosby-type exceptions, black folks on the home front are vocal and direct. Even when the voice isn't loud, it's strong. Most blacks—from 20 to 60—did not grow up in a household of "time outs" and "sit in the corner." Most of us grow up in households where if there were not outright ass whuppings, there were plenty of threats of them.

The words we grew up hearing were along the lines of "No, 'cuz I said so." "I brought you into this world, I can take you out." "You bet not." "Do what I said to do, not what you see me do." "Boy, if you do that one more time." "Girl, if you don't stop that right this minute." "Nunya—that stands for none of your business."

Clear. Simple. Direct. No room for ambiguity. Tons of drama, but plenty of clarity. When you broke a rule, you knew you were breaking one, and you knew there would be plenty to say on someone's part (not yours) if you got caught.

No, not all black people grew up that way. And yes, some folks who aren't black grow up that way.

Indirect Directness

In general, direct communication, even in very imperfect, dys-
functional households, is something that more black people are
familiar with than probably any other group of people. That's
why the more understated, if not downright passive-aggressive,
forms of communication that many whites engage in can create
absolute culture shock when blacks enter the work world popu-
lated by whites.

I've always informally made this observation as an employee.
As an attorney, I've seen how black folks can have even more of
a tendency to increase their directness and come off as con-
frontational when they encounter a problem at work. In general,
long before it gets to an employee filing a complaint or a lawsuit,
black employees don't deal with bad news with soft energy.

Even when the communication is not about conveying negative information, even during everyday conversation, the black
style of communication can be rattling to whites not used to it.

Because I am extremely direct, probably even more so than
the average black person, my style requires a bit of acclimation
for the whites who work with me. In many places I have worked
most of the whites actually find it a refreshing change of pace,
but my challenge (one I still struggle with) is learning when to
curb my directness so that what I'm trying to say doesn't get lost
in the style in which I say it.

I was happy to see that a study on cultural communication
(Toolkit for Cross-Cultural Collaboration, 1999) emphasized
what I had always observed about the different ways different
racial groups communicate. This study compared the different
communication styles of blacks, whites, Native Americans,
Asians, and Hispanics. Among the findings:

- Blacks communicate with much more animation and emotional expression than any other group.

- Blacks and Hispanics communicate with more gestures than other groups.

- Blacks speak with somewhat more volume than any other group. (To put it in my own words, energetically, we black people take up a lot of space.)

A driver brings his or her style of communication to the workplace with both the intention to speak and the intention to be heard. A driver knows that every time you open your mouth at work, or put words to paper or a computer screen, you drive either closer to your goals or further away from them.

In a company where no one but white males ran things, Jewel, a stylish and focused sister in her late 20s, had the executives regularly eating out of her French-manicured hands. Jewel got that a woman didn't need to sleep her way to the top; she just had to listen her way to the top. She listened carefully to how each executive spoke to her about job assignments, and when she spoke back, she mirrored their language and their tempo and listened for the hidden nuances of what they didn't say. For example, when dealing with the fidgety, high-tempo supervisors, Jewel spoke quickly and to the point; however, when dealing with the slower, more laid-back higher-ups, Jewel's cadence would be more like molasses, slow and sweet. Jewel had found that when you learn to match your pace to that of your speakers,

> they feel more comfortable with you, thus telling you more
> about how to meet their work needs.

Jewel is a driver whose communication style usually gets her exactly what she wants. Instead of doing one-size-fits-all work for each honcho, Jewel tailors her approach and her results to each person to maximize her relationship with each executive. Because Jewel listened well and mirrored—not mimicked—their styles of communication, she received their trust and they looked at her work with the expectation that it would provide what they required and more.

Where Jewel's particular gift lay was in recognizing that as a young, attractive black woman in heavily corporate America, she had to get right to the 85 percent similarity and dwell in that 15 percent difference zone no longer than she had to. Getting great credentials in the first place got her to the starting line, but talking her employers' language helped drive her to a winning finish.

Sounding White, Talking Black

We live in a society where we all know what the phrase "sounds black" means in reference to describing how someone speaks. If you're an educated black person who sounds as if you went to a predominantly white private or suburban public school while growing up, you know the sting of having another black person tell you that you "talk white."

Language is the most important way we define and describe ourselves, once we get past race and gender. Language, however, isn't just about words. The style of your words—your syntax, your degree of formality, your grammar, and more—becomes a form of communication, and that style can make or break you in the working world.

Martin, for example, was not having trouble with words when he went to his boss to get the thumbs-up on whether he should buy that car he had his eye on. They were both speaking the same language—no gaps in dialect, no great divide between understanding that when Martin said he wanted to buy a car he was actually asking about his job security. Jack understood exactly what Martin was asking, but only Jack knows why he chose the indirect route to deal with Martin. As a result, while Martin and Jack both spoke the same language (English with a Texas twang), they each used two distinct styles of communication.

Martin was really asking the question, "Look, man, I haven't been at this job long and I'm uncertain about how you feel about me. If you think I'm good at what I do, let me know. If you're having problems with my work, shoot me a hint or, better yet, tell me straight I'm not cutting it."

It was irrelevant that Martin was asking about buying a car. He could have mentioned buying a house, buying a puppy, proposing to his girlfriend. The point was that by tying his new purchase to concerns about his job, Martin was asking his boss to give him feedback before he sank money he couldn't afford into a new ride.

Because Martin was a friend of mine, he had confided in me, over the course of his employment, his sense that his boss wasn't impressed with his work or his work ethic. Therefore, it wasn't like he didn't have a clue that his job could have been on the line. I know that Jack's lack of directness was not entirely his fault. Martin was not good at reading his environment. While whites in general may not be as direct as blacks, if you pay attention, you can read when someone is being indirect loud and clear.

Jack had repeatedly made passing snide comments about Martin's failure to get to work on time. Jack had also commented a few times on problems he had with Martin's work. Martin may have thought he was being direct when he asked Jack about his performance, using the car purchase issue as a way to soften the question, but that's not effective, and Martin should have known that was not effective when Jack's response addressed the car purchase issue and did *not* address the performance issue. At that point, Martin should have more directly asked about his work performance or he should have just held off on buying the car until he got his official evaluation. In Martin's case, the 15 percent difference regarding that particular conversation might not have prevented him from losing his job in the first place, but it might have saved him acquiring a new car note until he got his next job.

A study done on *intercultural sensitivity* (how different ethnic groups understand each other and get along) by Milton Bennett shows that there are six stages of development. Although the model is based on the premise that whites are the ones who need to learn intercultural sensitivity, the model actually applies to a person of color trying to make his or her way in a workplace filled primarily with those from another culture.

The first stage is *denial*, where people do not recognize cultural differences. The second stage is *defense*, where people recognize some differences, but see them as negative. The third stage is *minimization*, where people are unaware of their projection of their own cultural values onto others and see their own values as superior. Stage four is *acceptance*, where people shift their perspective to understand that what they consider ordinary behavior can have different meanings in different cultures.

Adaptation, which is stage five, involves evaluating the behavior of people in a different cultural group from their frame of reference and adapting your behavior to fit what is normal in this different culture. The last stage of Bennett's theory is called *integration*, where people can shift their frame of reference and become comfortable with evaluating situations from multiple frames of references.

Bennett's theory is instructive because it points to the fact that when you enter a situation where the people are different from you, at some point you've got to adapt to the environment. While the environment may alter slightly because of the element that is different from the rest, it will basically remain the same.

Almost every black person has experienced a white person telling a story about some situation where the white person was in the minority—visiting a black neighborhood or a black church or a meeting where most of the people attending were black. It's always amusing to hear the awe in white people's voices when they talk about their walk on the other side. It's usually very amusing to hear their pride in stating how they adapted to a "foreign" environment that, at best, they stayed in for an hour or two, max. We as blacks hearing those stories get either mad at or amused by the fact that whites don't make the connection that our adaptation happens every day we go to work.

Denial Ain't Just a River in Africa

Denial isn't a problem blacks generally have when we enter the workforce. Our parents probably expend far more effort and time emphasizing how different white folks are from us than white folks do with their own kids about blacks. In both cases, the differences emphasized are usually negative and not necessarily based on fact. In a nutshell, you can't teach what you don't know, so sometimes what gets passed down from one generation to the next are just untested stereotypes. Teaching blind negativity does not result in helpful tools.

Blacks who are survivors, depending on why they are emphasizing survival, usually focus on how whites are similar. Whites who work with black survivors usually knock themselves out encouraging blacks who downplay their differences, allowing those blacks to emphasize similarities so that they don't have to step out of their comfort zones.

Strivers, like survivors, recognize the areas of similarity, but they emphasize select areas of similarity for strategic purposes. Although some may be clumsy at it while others are skilled, black strivers usually know full well what they're doing when they emphasize the right things in communication. For example, a striver, hearing that his boss likes tennis, might make a point of interjecting tennis news or information into their casual interactions to signal, "I should get points, because we like the same thing." This differs from a survivor in that the striver is consciously trying to better her position with that particular boss by emphasizing similarities rather than simply trying to blend in as much as possible, which is more of the survivor's motivation.

Thrivers normally don't think about the impact their communication has on whites, because they don't care. A thriver, however, would be better served by paying more attention to the results of his communication to see if that attitude really serves him, or where and when it does and doesn't. For example, if he finds his style of communication with his supervisor always leaves the supervisor acting defensive toward him, maybe that thriver needs to soften the way he communicates. In doing so, maybe he will increase his chances of getting more of what he wants and needs at work, from more money to better assignments to a more peaceful environment.

Blacks who are successful in the workplace know that communication and language are the key places where that 15 percent difference is most likely to rear its head. One of the ways a black person can minimize any difficulties in that respect is to do more listening than assuming.

One of the things I'm infamous for at work is getting witnesses to talk to me and tell me things no one else can get out of them. Young, old, black, white, accused, accusers, I just have this knack for getting people to feel comfortable with me and tell me more than they plan to.

From watching other people, particularly my white coworkers, conduct interviews, I think that what I do differently from most others that makes people more open with me is to not let my preconceived assumptions guide what I'm hearing. That allows me to hear what the person is saying, which leads to a better next question. For example, while I was interviewing a female employee who was accusing a male coworker of sexually harassing her, she mentioned in passing her friendship with another male coworker. Although seemingly irrelevant, some instinct told me to probe her on the nature of her friendship with the other male coworker. She stumbled around with the answer, but the bottom line was she had a sexual relationship with him, and he was a good buddy of the accused. While technically that didn't absolve her accused of liability, it put her accusations in a different light, which later resulted in the complaint being dropped.

My point is that most people would have been so focused on eliciting information regarding the person she was actually making the complaint against, they wouldn't have bothered to ask about something seemingly irrelevant. I guess even as an attorney, the newspaper reporter in me always is pushed to ask the next nosy-ass question. Most people are so assumption-drenched, they don't really hear other people. They hear the words, but not the point. They hear the emotion but they don't get the underlying concern. We all have a tendency to be more poised for rebuttal than we are open to hearing someone else's viewpoint.

In the workplace, from Day One, you have to listen to people and observe them without judgment. Studies say that most communication is nonverbal, and I believe that is true. Therefore, listening and watching the environment you work in is a way of better figuring out communication. In general, you do that by listening to what your coworkers talk about, reading your environment for the use of idiom and expression, and paying attention to the style in which people speak. For example, as an 85 percent issue, if you work in a place where people curse like sailors, a well-chosen expletive won't damn you (pardon the pun), but if you rarely hear cussing at work, and if you're aiming to be a driver, you might want to put a lid on that potty mouth in the office.

Just Bring Up Tiger

One of the things that you listen for in the workplace is what people talk about. The arrival of Tiger Woods probably did more to bridge any 15 percent differences in communication than any other sports figure. Suddenly, it became cool for a black person to come to work talking about golf without sounding like he was straining too hard to talk to whites.

Thrivers without a doubt will be the black employees who make the least allowance for different modes of communication by culture. A thriver will talk about the joys of Allen Iverson while everyone else salutes Tiger Woods. A thriver will say "dis" and "dat" to the CEO with the same straightforwardness with which she talks to the clerk in the mailroom.

Under the paradigm stated by Bennett, the thrivers will never get to stage six—integration. Well, that's not true. Thrivers may have the ability to integrate—recognize all the different ways to switch between cultures—but just choose not to do so. Again, my classifications are about motivation, not ability. I know of one brother, a partner at a major, predominantly white law firm, who was educated at great schools, but who deliberately turned up his black lingo around other white partners to force them to loosen up. He was instinctively a thriver; however, his success as a driver came from one, being stellar in his area of practice, and two, knowing when it was safer to trot out the black patois and when circumstances, such as meeting with a client or in court, required him to flash the Ivy League smile and speak King's English.

Code Switching

Code switching—the term used to describe being bicultural (operating simultaneously in two different cultures)—for most blacks in the workplace is just something we have to learn from the time we leave our parents' home to go out into the world. Another term I've heard used to describe code switching is *functional multilingualism*. An example of that is saying "excuse me" when you accidentally bump into a white coworker and reflexively saying "my bad" when you accidentally bump into a black coworker later that day. Granted, both of your coworkers might refer to you as a klutz, but that would just be an example of how most cultures intersect.

We all code switch to a certain degree. For example, in my home, I own a "refrigerator." When I go over to friends' homes, regardless of their race, if I'm in their kitchen, I refer to their "refrigerator." But when I walk into my grandmother's house and head for the kitchen, suddenly the only word I know for the electric contraption that holds cold food is "icebox." That's what I grew up hearing, that's what Cliffie (my grandmother) still calls it because of her generation, and that's the word I revert to when I visit her house. Code switching isn't just about race, it's about environment and reverting back to comfort and habit. That's why you'll be talking with a second generation coworker or friend who doesn't have a trace of an accent, and you'll see her get a call from a relative where she immediately falls into another language, and then hang up and, without missing a beat, resume her conversation in English with you. I love that! Unfortunately, when blacks do that, it's called by one of my least favorite words— Ebonics.

Language is such a rich, vivid part of who we are. Even the way we use the same words can say so much about a culture.

Cedric the Entertainer talks about how the difference between blacks and whites is the difference between wishing and hoping. Whites will run late for a concert saying, "I hope no one is sitting in our seats." Blacks will run late for a concert and say, "I wish someone would be sitting in our seats." Granted, on paper, it doesn't have the same tone, the same resonance, the same kick-ass attitude with which Cedric says it, but we all know what he means.

How We Say It Is How We Live It

The original title of my book was *Flavor in the Melting Pot: The Black Person's Guide to Employment in the White World*. The publishers changed it because they didn't think the title was descriptive enough for what the book is about. I agree; however, this expression is how I think of us—as the flavor that makes the melting pot stew richer, tastier.

There's a reason why black words and phrases make their way into everyday language. I think I fell off my couch the first time I heard a white character on television say "It's all good" like they grew up with some colored people. That's our stuff. Our words.

We know the phrases that unite us. Words like "If he had been black and done that" or "We can't keep nothing for ourselves." Black employees say those words whenever it applies or wherever they can say it without being overheard. Sometimes we don't have to say the words. We can just glance across a room during a meeting or across a piece of equipment at each other, and the words get said without speaking. We get tired of having to validate our experiences and so we keep it to ourselves, which just increases the conversations and the reactions we have behind the backs of whites. Understand that my point is not that these comments and conversations happen everyday, but, yep, they happen frequently and they happen regardless of class.

I think white coworkers, bosses, customers, and subordinates don't realize there are a whole host of words, phrases, and catchwords that form a universal sublanguage or shorthand. We all know what a "HNIC" (Head Nigga in Charge) is and we've all heard the adage about how we (meaning blacks) have to get up earlier in the morning to be able to go toe to toe with whites. And there is no question that we've heard about the "crabs in the bar-rel" syndrome where one black contends with other blacks try-ing to bring him down from success.

We, as black people, need to do the bilingual thing. To do that successfully we have to start really listening to how whites talk and communicate with each other. It also means that we have to pay attention to how whites don't communicate with each other.

If Martin were operating from survivor mode, his best bet would have been to just not ask his boss about his status and wait until he received his official evaluation. Survivors should assume that white managers will be as risk averse as they are toward direct confrontation, and for people who operate from a passive-aggressive posture, any conversation past "Hello, how are you doing today?" becomes a breeding ground for confrontation.

A striver probably would have asked in a less direct fashion. For example, a striver might have said, "Hey, Jack, I'm really inter-ested in getting feedback on my job performance and I'm inter-ested in knowing what role you see me playing in the future with this organization. Can we sit down and talk about that?" A striver would be operating with a dual agenda—the agenda of figuring out where he really stood with his boss while also gen-uinely wanting to know if he had enough job security to acquire a new debt.

A thriver probably wouldn't have asked at all because if he wanted a new car he would have bought one and he wouldn't have given the boss even the illusion he had any power over that decision.

Some things blacks just can't change overnight. Dialect is one of them. Me, I sound like a black woman from the Midwest, edu-cated in primarily white schools. Someone meeting me for the first time would guess that I'm educated, but they won't mistake me either for a preppie or as coming directly from the 'hood. If I tried to sound like either extreme, I would just sound silly. Because I work in the Midwest, my dialect isn't an issue.

How your accent or dialect sounds in the place you work is something that you need to be conscious of, if it is different from the rest. The bottom line is that as a black person, if you work in any kind of professional job, you have to get the basics of proper English down pat. Regardless of whether you are a survivor, a striver, or a thriver, you need to make sure your subjects and verbs agree in a sentence when you speak. If you're in the habit of a dissing and datting too much (translation: mispronouncing "this" and "that"), you need to get it under control. You need to be bilingual enough to control it when you're at work at least.

Communication is also more than how you say things; it's also the subjects you choose to talk about. The following is my list of no-no topics at work, no matter what type of employee you are:

- Any white artist accused of stealing from black pop culture
- Affirmative action
- Politics
- Whether O.J. did it or not
- Welfare
- Poverty
- Crime
- Living in the suburbs (unless you're a black who lives in the suburbs)
- Anything relating to sex
- The problem with racial profiling

I could list about 10 other off-limits topics, but everyone has to use his own judgment based on his particular job. You may be wondering what you can talk about. Until you know your environment and the boundaries you have with individual coworkers, safe, nonwork topics include sports, pop culture events, nonpolitical news events, general family topics, and the weather. The weather is *always* a safe topic.

Regardless of whether you are a survivor, striver, or thriver, here are some principles that can help you to succeed with workplace communication and keep any 15 percent difference issues to a minimum.

First of all, while there are some jobs that don't involve any writing at all (such as manual labor jobs), being particularly conscious of writing well is a necessity. When you write e-mails, memorandums, anything, you have to demonstrate your grasp of English. It may be an unfair standard, but we can't afford to appear any more uneducated than some stereotypes indicate that we are, particularly if we are strivers or work in any kind of job where a degree is required. If you think you have problems with basic writing, you should hunt out a friend you trust and who you think is a good writer and ask for help. If you're uncomfortable with that approach, buy a book on good writing or take a class at the community college. The important issue is not whether white folks think you're a good writer, but whether you have the confidence to know that you are communicating at your best at all times.

Most word processing programs allow you to check the spelling and grammar on documents. Do it. Do it before you send an e-mail so that even if you don't sound overly educated, you at least come off as careful—an extremely important attribute to be known for, no matter what your job is. In addition to spell check, keeping a dictionary or a thesaurus handy is also a good idea.

Another tip is to observe how the people around you communicate, especially the people who have the greatest impact on your job. Listen to how people talk to others, and then compare that to what they say when those people aren't around. Observe who your bosses go out of their way to talk to when it is not directly job related, and objectively pay attention to why. Don't just get caught up in the knee-jerk reaction of "My white boss only talks to white people" because usually it isn't that simple. I once made that assumption about a boss. He is a white male in his 50s, and at social events I noticed that he appeared to go out of his way to talk only to the other white men. It used to really piss me off, but when I stepped back and thought about it, I noticed that it wasn't all the white males that he talked to. So I started paying greater attention to his conversations with the white males he did talk to. What I noticed was that his main topic of conversation with them was sports, and that the white males he didn't talk to were not big sports fans. Bingo! Well, after I started throwing the occasional sports metaphor into my conversation and striking up chats about certain sporting events, he began loosening up around me and we started having a better, more open working relationship in general.

Now granted, my initial instinct was right—he gravitated more toward white men because his unstated bias was that those guys would have more in common with him, but my objective was to have a better working relationship with him, not to undo 50 years of bias that existed before he met me.

After you've observed your environment, act accordingly. If you are a big user of slang and you see that does not happen much where you work, keep it to a minimum, except for conversations with coworkers you're very tight and personal with. It's also important to moderate your pitch and tone. If you work in a dry, low-key environment, then don't be the loudest person in the room. (I've always had trouble with that one, too, but life is easier when I do pay attention and attempt to bring it down a notch in those environments.) Trust me, if you're black and you're loud when everyone else is a soft talker, somehow that will bite you in the butt.

You also need to know what *not* to communicate. Unless you work in an environment where the nature of the job involves openly talking about racial issues, as a black person, it's just best to stay away from such *scary* conversations at work. (My definition of scary is any topic that draws attention to the fact that you're black and other people in the room aren't.) It's a no-win situation. Now granted, if you're a thriver, accustomed to doing things your way without regard to perception, then it doesn't matter. If the water cooler discussion turns to how *Seinfeld* is one of the greatest television shows ever made and you want to point out that you don't understand how a show demonstrating life in New York City doesn't have any black folks in it, bring it on— but when the discomfort level suddenly turns icy, know that's the chance you take.

Communication is one of the most important ways you need to attend to your 15 percent issues if you want to successfully get yours and get ahead at work. If you train yourself to read your environment on automatic pilot, however, it's easier than you think.

5

HAIR, FLAIR, AND WHAT YOU WEAR

■

Mark pledged Omega Psi Pi fraternity when he was an undergrad at the University of Everybody's Business. Just about every black college student knows that part of pledging Omega Psi Pi, also known as the Qs, may mean more than handing over your money and wearing purple and gold. As part of his "going over" (as pledging is called), Mark got the infamous "Q" branded on his arm. Branded. Hot iron. Imprinted, bold and huge, on the bicep of his right arm. The brand may not take up much space, but there's no avoiding it once you see his bare arm.

Fast forward a few years later to when this young, upstanding brother was a second-year law student, clerking for the summer at a conservative, all-white law firm.

Mark found himself invited to several swimming pool party events—the kind of socializing that is particularly important for black folks so that the people who are hiring can figure out if you know how to use the right fork in front of clients, or make appropriate small talk without embarrassing yourself or the firm.

Needless to say, Mark didn't get in the pool that summer. He made sure his T-shirts carefully covered his beloved brand. Covering up the brand was physically not that hard to do. The average sleeve on a T-shirt covers up the brand. Unfortunately, his nervousness while trying to make sure no one saw the brand at all those outdoor "casual" firm events made Mark seem standoffish and socially inept.

Mark did a good job that summer, however, he wasn't offered a full-time position when the summer was over.

Moral of the story? Don't try to get a job at an all-white law firm if you're not white? No. Don't join fraternities or sororities that require body parts to be altered or permanently imprinted? Well, that would get into my personal opinion. The true moral of the story is that, like communication, physical appearance is something that all workers need to be concerned with. It can also be one of the first areas to see the 15 percent factor creep in.

Part of being black in the white workplace involves understanding that you may be the first and only black that your coworkers, bosses, and subordinates deal with on a daily basis. From the day you start, it doesn't take a psychic to read which of your white workmates deal with blacks up close and personal only when they are at work.

That's why appearance can be a form of communication. We judge other people, whether fairly or not, by how they carry themselves. For example, we draw different conclusions about a woman who has six pairs of holes in her ears versus a woman who only wears clip-on pearl earrings. Even a person who has no idea who Lil' Kim is will not look at a picture of her and assume she's a schoolteacher. More likely, a person seeing a picture of Lil' Kim wearing an outfit tight, bright, and see-through would appropriately guess that she was an entertainer.

Appearance can be our calling card. Never is that more important than when interviewing for a job. While being yourself is important, presenting that self in the best light should be your number one priority.

The basics always apply:

- Make sure you look clean and neat.

- Don't wear an outfit to an interview that you would wear to a nightclub.

- Gum in any flavor or mode of chewing is out.

- Ball caps or tennis shoes aren't for the office.

- Try to limit your aroma to soap, because you never know when your interviewer has a perfume or cologne allergy.

- There is no such thing as "off the record" when it comes to job hunting. Even if you're just going to pick up an application or drop off a letter of reference, make sure your appearance reflects your serious interest in the job.

Once, when I was in the office of a human resources manager during the investigation of a case I worked on, a brother
came in off the street to ask for a job application. I couldn't see
the man from where I was sitting, but I could hear the disdain in
the manager's voice as she asked him questions and gave him an
application. The manager, a young black woman, told me that it
annoyed her when black people came in for an application looking "any ol' way." Apparently the young man must have worked
at a job that involved plenty of dark, oily grease because his body
and his clothes were smudged all over with it.

While that young man may have stopped for an application
during the only time he could—on his way home from the job he
already had—his appearance worked against him. You don't have
to dress up as if you are meeting the CEO on every encounter,
but until you have the starting date of a new job, assume that
every appearance you make counts. (And don't ever discount the
people who work in human resources, because what they lack in
power, they usually make up for in influence and access when
you're trying to get the job in the first place.)

Like any other group, we take for granted that our style of doing
things is something that everyone knows about. For example, we
assume that everyone knows that we don't have to wash our hair
every day. We assume that when we say we're going to get a per-
manent that means our hair comes back straighter, not curlier as
it means with whites. We take for granted that when we're invited
to a party and told that the dress is casual, that means we go a
little tighter, a little brighter, and definitely a little bolder.

Never underestimate how the language of dress screams. If you wear orange every day in a sea of blue suits, you signal more than that you like the color orange. You show your employers that you are bold, original, and unconventional. Look at the cues around you, however. If no one else is being bold, you might stand out as eccentric. At the very least, if you're going to wear the orange every day over your black skin, you better excel beyond the best of the blue suits at what you do. That's where researching your environment before you get the job becomes especially necessary.

Once you get an interview, use that as your opportunity to pay careful attention to the appearance of the people at the company. Note if hairdos are conservative or funky. Observe if clothes are sedate or stand out. Watch to see if people wear offbeat jewelry or strictly stick to Timex and gold studs. Being aware of these things when you interview will show you if more than just your wardrobe clashes with your work environment.

Let's get back to Mark for a minute. First of all, let's ask, was he trying to survive, strive, or thrive?

Assume that Mark was trying to survive. When you're clerking for the purpose of getting a job, your only real goal is getting the job offer at the end of the proverbial rainbow. You can pretend in your mind that if you get the job you can start on your first day of work wearing a five-foot-high Afro and a "No Justice, No Peace" T-shirt, and greet all your coworkers with an appropriate Muslim greeting. (You *know* you're not going to do that, but little mental daydreams like that may be what get you through the rough spots.) As someone aiming to survive, it would be smart for Mark to wear a T-shirt over his brand, keep a low profile, and take his chances. There was no way, when he was spending the summer trying to get a job, that he needed to have

conversations with white folks on why a black man would willingly get himself branded. Any conversation a black person gets
himself into at work that even remotely touches on slavery (as
branding would) is a no-win situation.

Now, say Mark was trying to strive—get the job offer, *but*
not feel like he had to hide in the shadows to do so. If that were
the case, then Mark's approach would be a little different. One,
he probably would still just keep the T-shirt on for all outdoor
events. But as someone striving, he would probably have a personality that allowed him to court the white folks a little bit
more. In other words, he would reach out more to get to know
folks individually, take the extra time to strike up a conversation
on the things he had in common with others, so that people paid
less attention to the fact that he was not jumping his seminaked
butt in the pool.

On the other hand, if Mark were trying to thrive, well, then
he probably wouldn't have to boost his T-shirt collection before
his clerkship started. He probably would not care what the white
folks thought, because his loyalty to his fraternity or just his own
sense of integrity about not hiding anything about himself would
rule. It would still be wise for Mark, Q brand and all, to extend
himself and explain his fraternity's philosophy about the branding and why members willingly subject themselves to a hot iron.
There will be that slice of white folks who will find it fascinating and educational, and might even bond with Mark as they
bring up their own crazy college antics. Then there will be that
group of white folks who won't have the guts to get into an actual
discussion with Mark about it, will write him off as a radical
Negro or ex-gang member, and they'll either keep him from getting the job or be a problem once he gets it anyway.

One thing is for sure. Whether Mark aimed to survive, strive, or thrive, lying is never an option in the workplace, especially for blacks. In a nutshell, Mark's options were to cover up his brand, reframe how the brand came about, or just refuse to talk about it and hope for the best.

There are two reasons why I don't suggest lying, even about something as seemingly minor as a fraternity symbol. I'm a believer in operating with integrity at all times. If you wanted to be a Q dog more than you wanted air to breathe when you were in college, then you shouldn't be ashamed of the fact that you were willing to get a brand. Discreetly hiding it from your employers is not the same as hiding it from yourself, which is what you do when you lie about it. We've all got things from our past that we are either ashamed of or, at the very least, not proud of, and lying about an aspect of your past is just too high a price to pay for getting any job. When you get your dream job, as a black person, you don't want any skeletons jumping out of your closets, even little bitty skeletons. This same analysis applies whether we're talking about a brand, tattoo, piercing, or hair style—anything that you can't hide or don't want to hide for personal reasons.

As a person who practices employment law I can advise you not to lie because lies almost always come to light. Stick to the high road, then if you ever have to pursue any action against your boss you have truth on your side and you don't have to worry about your credibility flushing your case down the toilet. Bottom line is, blacks just don't have the option to have credibility issues in the workplace. Even an empty lie, such as saying that your fraternity brothers wrestled you to the ground and gave you the brand, has a way of catching up with you. When I worked as a newspaper reporter I learned that there is always someone who knows the truth to any lie you tell. And as a lawyer who has investigated discrimination lawsuits, I've learned that there is always someone willing to tell that truth under oath in a deposition.

One aspect about dress that many people, blacks in particular, don't think about is that while how you carry yourself communicates who you are and what you want, the way employees dress and conduct their grooming to a certain extent communicates the objective of the employer.

Take McDonald's, for example. We do more than recognize those golden arches. No one would deny McDonald's has the right to require employers to wear uniforms to work, with no significant deviations. We would all probably agree that the company has the right to convey a unified corporate image so that people get the same comfort level whether they're at a Mickey D's in Rochester, New York, or Rolla, Missouri, or Riverside, California.

Even in an environment where uniforms are not required, companies have the right to set a standard and a tone that conveys a certain type of professionalism. While blacks have brought lawsuits against their employers for grooming policies that they felt were discriminatory, such as prohibiting black men from wearing beards to cover up keloid scars or black women from wearing braids (other than when Bo Derek made them fashionable, that is), that's a hard road to go down if your bottom line is to keep your job. Besides, it's easier to complain about a policy prohibiting bushy Afros than a policy that prohibits you from wearing your Bootsy Collins and P-Funk concert T-shirt to work as an accountant.

If you want to be a driver, you need to make grooming choices that are not just about your personal taste but about maximizing the image you present to anyone you meet as an employee—whether customer, client, vendor, stockholder, or member of the public. Even when you don't have hard-and-fast rules to follow, make the choices that not only make you look good but make you look good in the way it really counts.

Fred is a brother who has been a newspaper reporter for almost 15 years. On any given day Fred could be called to any assignment, at any time, in any part of the city. When it came to how he presented himself physically, Fred was a driver right down to his polished shoes. He knew that to convince anyone to talk to an unknown black man, he needed to wear clothes that put people at ease. Fred found that a tie, pressed shirt, and khakis or suitable dress pants (plus a reporter's notebook) usually eased his way through any threshold.

Sure, there were times when Fred wanted to skip the tie or not pull out the iron. There were times when Fred wanted to wear a T-shirt to beat the heat or a sweatshirt that was comfy when it was too damn cold. There were days when he just plain didn't feel like pulling out the razor. But he knew those weren't options. He put himself in charge of driving his career forward, and he knew that the first time a source or witness refused to be interviewed by him because she was wary of his appearance, the burden would be on him to explain to his bosses why he didn't get the story.

Of course, there were times when people didn't speak to Fred anyway—that's a professional hazard for any journalist—but Fred knew that his appearance was his first calling card, even before he identified himself, and he couldn't afford ever to forget that if he wanted front-page news stories, he needed always to look the part.

The key issue is awareness. You have to be aware that apparent differences merit discussion, conversation, and spotlights. Sometimes you feel like being an educator, sometimes you don't. One of the realities is that our uniqueness in being black and our desire to be unique among our brothers and sisters sometimes makes our grooming a topic of conversation.

Mary the J.D., my friend at work, made some changes over a six-month period of time: she went from having her hair as short as Halle Berry, to having shoulder-length braids à la Brandy, to hair that was Toni Braxton straight when Toni was in her long-mane phase. Did girlfriend care what the white folks thought about the fact that she went through almost as many looks as Mary J. Blige does between the Grammys and the Soul Train Music Awards? Nope. But the important thing my friend was aware of before she did it is that the one thing that merits more attention than difference is change. Therefore, Mary the J.D. was prepared for the attention, and she knew that her work environment was relaxed enough to accept personal expression. She knew all of this *before* she made the changes, so that she could smoothly and appropriately handle any hair-focused discussions.

Mary the J.D. also kept the topic of her hair care off the debating team schedule in the first place. I've seen my African American sisters launch loud campaigns about their color, cut, or addition to their hair while at work. Unfortunately, some of us give the appearance of putting more thought into our hair and our clothes than we do into our jobs or our career. An overstatement? Look at the facts. African Americans spend three times as much on cosmetics as the rest of America. Yep. We spend money looking good, and as part of looking good, we draw attention to ourselves. That's great, because a sister doesn't put on a hot new lip color to not look good. A brother does not have his barber shave him just right for his look to not look tight.

White people like to look good, too. I know of one white coworker who is legendary for going to the barber to get his hair trimmed more often than most of us floss our teeth. That's not the point. The point is that success in the workplace requires that more attention be paid to how well you do your job than how fashionable you look doing it. We, by the very nature of being black in the workplace, generate more attention, and one thing we all know is that, for some reason, what we do gets blown up to the size of a big-screen television when we do it.

Anna has a small tattoo on the inside of one of her wrists. She had a great interview with her employer but, for reasons unknown to Anna, the employer required a background check based on concern that the tattoo might represent a wild past that could have negative implications if she got the job. She didn't have a wild past. She just had a tattoo—not the most strategically placed tattoo for someone climbing the corporate ladder, but, hey, for that particular job, it caused no more than a short delay and a questionable invasion of her privacy that she never found out about.

So, what's the answer? You've got to wear clothes to work. Your hair has to look some way. Tattoos or fraternity brands may already be part of your personal mix.

If you're a survivor the answer is to keep it simple and keep it silent. This means that you keep your experimental hairdos and attention-grabbing styles for the weekend or vacation, or until you reach the point in your career where you really don't care. Regardless of what you do, you observe what the corporate culture looks like, and follow it as closely as your sun-kissed skin can comfortably get away with. Keep your grooming tips out of the workplace. If you work in a khaki-wearing, blue-shirt-sporting fashion palace, you break out the Dockers and act happy about it.

If you're a striver and want to make your professional mark on the workplace while imbuing it with your own personal style, I still say keep it silent. Be fashionably elegant or breakout beautiful, but always keep the focus on how well you do your job and how good your work results are, and let your personal style just be one of those things that people notice without attracting undue attention.

The question for those who don't want to compromise and don't want to be a slave to corporate culture is to just be aware of the consequences. For example, I have had dreadlocks for the past two years. Many a jaw has dropped when the attorney representing not the person bringing the lawsuit, but rather the company being sued, is the black woman with dreadlocks and a nontraditional work outfit.

I take the chance every day that some judge, some client, some witness, some person I work with jumps to some sort of judgment about me based on my "radical" hairstyle. For me it's worth it because I really like my hair. Now, when I worked at the second-biggest law firm in the same city, my hair was permed and straight as a bone. There was no way my behind would even have gotten the job with any hairstyle that screamed ethnic. Would they have told me that's why I didn't get the job? Hell, no. I did work for lawyers. Would they have intentionally discriminated against me if I had started growing the locs while I was there? As a corporation, no. But there would be some individual I worked for whose perception of me would change, and while the law does prohibit discrimination, it doesn't prohibit negative perceptions. That may be a fuzzy line, but it's the fuzzy line we live with. (See Chapter 9 for more on this topic.)

The point of this chapter isn't really about fraternity brands or hairstyles. It's about how we wear our selves—our true selves—and how that plays in the workplace.

A client I worked for, an employer of a large entry-level workforce, some time ago took a survey of its employees to design a fair dress code policy, so that the company didn't inadvertently fail to take into account some issue they hadn't considered. What the survey revealed is that the young black female employees had much different standards of what was appropriate to wear to work than the white female employees. The black women didn't have as much problem with lower necklines and higher hemlines. At least at this workplace, with those particular employees, flashing a little T and A wasn't such a bad thing. That particular employer cared enough about fairness to adjust its policies to take into account cultural and generational differences. Most employers don't. They have rules and standards that they expect employees to follow and the boss is not too good about custom-fitting the standard.

The main issue for us is awareness. The second issue is choice. The order of those two things is important. My mother is a high school graduate who has worked for the federal government for more than 30 years and has been promoted about a jillion times, gaining more supervision and responsibility with every move. My mom is way ahead of me—starting with less and doing one heck of a lot more. One of her favorite responses when I tell her that this person did this or that person did that is to just to say, "Choices. Everybody has them."

Awareness and choice go hand in hand in the workplace. Be aware of the possible outcomes or perceptions that result from the choices you make. Being aware will help you evaluate your choices ahead of time so that you don't react to a given situation without forethought.

Lenny, an attorney, told me he would love to loc his hair, but he wouldn't because of the impact he feared this particular hair choice would have on his clients. Lenny's rationale was that while people may accept locs from a black female trial attorney as nothing more than a hairstyle choice, with a black man it would come across as some sort of social statement. Lenny demonstrated the power of how awareness must come before choice. In his case, he knew that he was not going to take a chance on something that would hurt not only him, but also his clients. As a trial attorney in a fairly conservative and racially divided city, Lenny was aware that, while he had the choice to wear his hair any way he wanted, he had to read his environment well enough to decide how much he was and wasn't willing to risk to make a personal choice.

Lenny wasn't an employee, since he had his own law firm, but even he knew that he had to play to his audience if he wanted success. Playing to his audience meant being aware of what would be acceptable, then making a choice based on that. At work, your audience is your boss, your coworkers, and your customers or clients.

A young black woman, Gina, called a colleague of mine, also a black employment lawyer, a few years ago to ask her if it was illegal for Gina's boss to tell her that the skirts she wore to work were too short. Gina just knew my friend was going to tell her, "Hell no, he can't do that! This is America, damn it, and he has no right to tell you what you can and can't wear. He's violating your civil rights. Let's sue the bastard!"

Instead, what Gina got was my colleague telling her that as an at-will employee her boss had the right to enforce an across-the-board, nondiscriminatory dress code that prevented employees from wearing clothes that were unduly distracting and thus inappropriate for the workplace.

Now my personal style, as opposed to that of my fellow sister litigator, would be to tell Gina something along the lines of, if you show up at a conservative insurance company every day showing more leg than a Popeye's Chicken Snack Pack, then maybe you shouldn't be surprised that your boss says something to you about putting more clothes on. But that's my style.

Anyway you slice it, if Gina was more aware that her hemline was quite a bit shorter than every other woman's at work, then maybe she would have made a better choice, rather than having her boss call her out about something that could have been avoided. Now, you may say at this point, maybe Gina wasn't trying to survive or even strive. Maybe Gina was trying to thrive. That's a good point, but that's why reading your environment is the key to success in your workplace. In Gina's environment, wearing buttcrack-high skirts may have been the breaking point where her individualism came head-to-head with the boss's ideal of workplace attire. Bottom line was, Gina was not the boss. She could crow all she wanted to about how it wasn't fair, but in the end it wasn't her call to make. Her choices were to get another job, break her own fashion rules and wear longer skirts, or take it to a higher authority at work and let them decide. Calling an attorney was her way of figuring out what her options were. Gina was counseled that if she chose to go over her supervisor's head, that path is going to put the spotlight not just on her hemline, but on her entire performance.

One thing you should look at when you accept a new job is if there is a dress code outlined in the company handbook. A company is not legally required to have a dress code policy (actually a company doesn't even have to have a company handbook, but most do), but if they do, then you aren't going to have much room for deviation.

■

Whether whites want to admit it or not, when blacks show up in the workplace what we do, say, or wear takes on big-screen Technicolor drama while what every other employee does, says, or wears gets displayed on the 13-inch screen.

If you're aware, then you pay attention to your environment and you make choices about where you as a black person fit in and what you accomplish in that environment. Whether your goal is to survive, strive, or thrive, isn't that what it's all about—doing well and living well while you're doing it?

In a nutshell, blacks do our "stuff" differently. We bring not just race but *color* to the workplace—different hair colors, bright colors, sharp colors, the colors of the rainbow, and the vivid colors of our minds. Awareness of how we look doing it is just another layer we constantly need to evaluate in our pursuit of cash and career.

6

FRIENDS, FOES, AND FAKERS

■

Todd, a black computer software engineer, was home sick for three days. The only time he left his apartment was to see the doctor and go to the pharmacy to get the medicine that his doctor prescribed for him.

Todd was having trouble with his boss, Jessica, a white female. He was the only black male in his department, and he was fairly sure that his direct, slightly abrasive style of talking clashed routinely with Jessica's gentle, laid-back Southern-fried charm and mode of speaking. Wayne, an older black supervisor from the human resources department whom he only knew in passing, called Todd to his office the day he got back from his illness. Todd was puzzled because there was no work-related reason for Wayne to talk to him and they never rolled together socially. When he arrived at Wayne's office, out of the blue Wayne said, "Man, if you're going to lie and call in sick, at least make it look good and stay at home in case someone calls." Todd was stunned.

Apparently, Jessica had gone to Wayne to report her suspicion that Todd was faking his illness. Wayne volunteered to call Todd at home to check on her suspicion. The only problem with that scenario was that Wayne happened to call during the two-hour block of time Todd was visiting his doctor and getting his prescription filled—something he figured out when Todd angrily showed him the three bottles of medication his doctor ordered him to take for the next two weeks.

Wayne had told Jessica that Todd probably didn't answer his phone because he was sleeping. He thought he had done Todd a favor.

Although some people are more social than others, the bonds you form at work can be the key not just to your success but also to your contentment. Whether you're a survivor, a striver, or a thriver, it makes the day go easier if the people you have to deal with are people you like and trust.

If you ever watched the television show *Survivor*, where people are stuck on an island and the last one standing wins one million dollars, then you know as the number of people dwindles down, the folks on the show love to talk about alliances. It's all a game of keeping track of who seems to be in whose pocket. The fascinating aspect is watching the alliances shift as each person gets closer to that million dollars. In the beginning, while a person's alliance might be to the person who can best catch a fish, it starts getting more about which of the people remaining you think you can beat.

The workplace is a lot like the game of *Survivor*—minus the island, eating bugs for lunch, and having a shot at a million dollars. It is an environment where you have to negotiate personal politics on a daily basis.

Most workers deal with camaraderie issues—who to befriend, who to enjoy, and who to eat lunch with. That's a basic 85 percent issue. A black survivor will be the least concerned with giving thought to her alliances. If the survivor isn't of the loner variety, a survivor will ally with anyone who crosses her path regularly and shows consistent pleasantness.

Strivers, because they are more focused on trying to get ahead, pick allies a bit more strategically. A black striver either is or should be allied with the people who have the biggest potential to take her where she wants to go. It isn't about using people —using people is when you pretend to like people you don't for no other reason than to get some advantage you wouldn't otherwise have. Strategically making friends and allies in the workplace is a matter of getting to know people slowly, and from there deciding how a bond between the two of you can work best.

The thrivers, black employees who have their own irrepressible style, make allies similar to the way survivors do—neither pays a whole lot of attention to picking the *right* people to know or the appropriate people to bond with. In general, thrivers tend to operate from more of a gut-level instinct on who to hang with at work and who not to. Once, when doing witness interviews at a company, I talked with a young black man who was close friends with an older white coworker who was known for saying the word *nigger* occasionally and making off-color jokes. When I asked the brother why he was so tight with the guy, he simply said, "I like him; he's real." Talking some more with the young man, he told me that he liked his white coworker because he always knew where he stood with the man and, in general, the man had his back. That is definitely a thriver way of looking at workplace friendships.

Alliances in the workplace are not monochromatic. As tempting as it may be, it would be a mistake to enter a new job and decide that all the black people are your friends, all the white people are your enemies, and everyone else should be judged by whether they seem to take the side of blacks or whites. This overly simplistic analysis will get you into trouble every time.

Even though I've said that most blacks in the workplace are either survivors, strivers, or thrivers, the reality is that on some level we are all survivors trying to figure out the optimal way to do our jobs each day. We all want to love the career path we're on and enjoy the rest of our lives when we're not on the clock. Except for a rare chosen few, we don't live to work, we work to live.

However, while most of us don't live to work, it matters who we share the bulk of our workdays with—whether they are people we enjoy, trust, and respect; whether they are people who validate us, or at the very least don't invalidate us.

So, how does a black employee pick alliances in the workplace? If you're smart, hopefully you can start before you even begin the job. Picking alliances is the one area of the work experience where being a driver doesn't come into play so much. While you can aim to be smart about who you trust and who you align yourself with, you can only be so calculated about making those choices.

I think it was General Patton who said that taking a calculated risk is not the same thing as being rash. However, when it
comes to friends and allies in the workplace, you may end up
being rash because you can't factor in, and therefore cannot control, the human element—that is, the human element of just hitting it off with some people more than others. Sure, you can try
to pick the *right* people to ally yourself with at work, but your
pickings exist without any input from you.

I'd like to think that I'm as close as anyone I know to being
a driver when it comes to alliances. I never underestimate the
importance of anyone; therefore, my plate of friends and associates at work has always been large. As I said earlier in the book,
being a driver is about the conscious choices you make, rather
than the instinctive ones you make as a survivor, striver, or
thriver. If you consciously choose your friends, you are increas-
ing your chance of success at work by making it a better and
more trusting place to be.

The reason you choose, whether survivor, striver, or thriver,
is that if you stand out, you want to know if you stand alone.
It's always dangerous to walk into a work situation assuming
who will or won't have your back. I like the old saying "the
enemy of my enemy is my friend" because it is a reminder of the
importance of knowing how people are connected. This is sometimes the most powerful piece of information you have. When
I was a reporter and covered a beat, I learned that the quickest
way to find out information was to figure out how it flowed.
You figured that out by figuring out the real ties that bind. If I
know (despite the fact that it isn't public knowledge) that City
Councilmember Sue hates the mayor but is best buds with Councilmember Frank who is super tight with City Planner Marco,

the best person to go to for background on possible budget cuts will probably be Councilmember Frank's secretary. Why? Because Frank will know the dirt from hanging out with Sue and the implications from chilling with Marco, and Frank's secretary will usually be the unconnected, accidental witness to what her boss knows. In simpler terms, to keep up with what's affecting your work world, you need to know who has pertinent information and the direction that information flows. But your first few days on a new job, there's no way you'll know these subtleties.

Additionally, whether you like it or not, as a black person you directly or indirectly have a relationship with every other black person who works at that place. From Day One, you will be judged, and for the most part, your harshest critics on the issue of alliances will be your black coworkers. You'll be judged by how you speak to other blacks, what blacks you don't speak to, which blacks you become friends with, and which ones you don't. If you become friends or allies with coworkers who aren't black, the trustworthiness of those relationships will be judged by how you relate to your black coworkers.

Black Like Me

We black people are a communal lot. When enough of us get together, even as total strangers, we can make any event a prayer meeting, a fight, or a party depending on who, what, when, and where. That's one of the reasons why, when blacks enter a new work situation, we usually do an automatic gut check on what's up with the other blacks who work there—to figure out who to be cool with and who to avoid like the Jerri curl.

In the summer of 2002 I was one of about 40 people anxiously waiting in line on the first day to purchase tickets to a Luther Vandross concert. In that short 45-minute event, the whole microcosm of how black people get along was clear—you saw shouting, raucous laughter, anger, suspicion, folks cussing over love and money, instant bonding of friends, and enemies about to be formed. You saw the whole theater of white people at the ticket booth rolling their eyes, the sister girl brought in from the back to tame the unruly masses, and plain good spirited unruliness—with just enough order and organization to keep it from breaking out into a straight up fight worthy of calling in the police. By the time the last person in line bought her ticket (while steadily complaining about the cost of the ticket and how far back her seats were), all was right with the world. Strangers became friends, vowing to look for each other at the concert. People who hadn't seen each other in a while caught up on old times and exchanged new numbers. The sister chastised by the group for not saving a place for a stranger who needed to run to the ATM was welcomed back into the fold. And the white ticket sellers looked relieved and surprised it all ended so well. It was loud. It was colorful. It didn't make no damn sense, and yet it moved in perfect order. It was so wonderfully black.

In the workplace, black people work a lot of the theater found in that concert line into our jobs. It's more like a soap opera than a feature film, but the dynamics are the same.

I mention the Luther Vandross ticket story as an example of how the energy changes when several black people get together. Except for the most bourgeois of black folks at a black-tie event, when blacks start interacting in groups, we can't help but get boisterous. Even if our voices don't get louder than a whisper, we shake things up when we get together.

What makes the workplace such a soap opera sometimes is that most people crave the sameness and the repetitiveness of human events. In foreign environments, especially ones that are somewhat threatening, you look for patterns, sameness, themes, anything that reminds you of territory you've walked before. This is an 85 percent issue—one all workers can relate to.

Workplace Politics

There are certain phrases that always make me cringe whenever I hear them, and I always mentally correct the phrases in my head. In the context of the workplace, one of them is when I hear someone say, "My job doesn't have workplace politics." Because I have a big mouth, I usually don't just keep my thoughts to myself. I usually say that even if only three people work together, workplace politics kick in whenever one of the three leaves the room.

Workplace politics are about alliances, viewpoints, opinions, knowledge, information, power, and how all those things intersect and play off each other. The natural thing for any person to do when he enters a foreign environment is to look for a home. You look for what makes you feel comfortable and safe. You look for the person you can take your cues from. Just like a visitor setting foot in a strange country, no matter how much you've studied the native language, the second you hear an American voice, you don't feel quite so alone.

Because, like everyone else, I like to be comforted in a new environment and I like to get a sense of who to befriend and from whom to run, my standard mental checklist whenever I start a new job is probably a lot like other black folks'. In no particular order:

- Where's the bathroom?

- Where do I get my coffee?

- Where is my boss's office in relation to mine?

- Where are the other black folks?

I've only had one job where there were no other black employees and it was no coincidence that it was one of the worst jobs I've ever had.

The assumptions, however, can get you into trouble if you go to work assuming that all other black people operate from the same place you do. I'm sorry to go there, but we all know that some of the most unreasonably stubborn, judgmental people in the history of thinking can be black folks who know what they know, and know how other blacks should behave.

In the example at the beginning of the chapter, Todd was dealing with an age-old truism of working while black—the HNIC. Wayne was the company's Head Nigger in Charge. It's a concept widespread and well known as crabs in the barrel. You know that syndrome? Where one black climbs up the ladder of success (the crab) and his fellow black coworkers (the other crabs) scramble like crazy to bring him back down with the rest of them, back into the barrel. God forbid one of them gets out if the rest of them can't all get out at the same time. It seems to me that the HNIC is the crab at the top of the barrel policing the rim to kick the other crabs right back to the bottom of the barrel. Or at least trying to, anyway.

In the example above, Wayne wasn't being nothing more than an HNIC. The second Jessica came to him with some bull-crap about not believing that Todd was really out sick, instead of playing "I Spy," Wayne should have merely told Jessica to request medical documentation from Todd when he returned. Even then she should only do that if it were her policy with every other employee in her department who was out sick for more than a day or two. Otherwise, Wayne is just participating in the workplace version of black-on-black crime. What does an HNIC gain at work for taking such action? It's today's spin on being a house nigger versus being a field slave—a black or a set of blacks always strive for the "in" slot with the whites in charge at the expense of other blacks.

The HNIC is usually the first black, who is still around, to have worked with the employer. Other times, it's the black employee who makes the most money or has the highest title. In some ways, it is probably less prevalent in the workplace today than it was 20 or 30 years ago when there were more real "firsts."

When you suspect a person you work with may be an HNIC, the best way to deal with her is like the elderly aunt in your family who you don't really like but who you go out of your way to be nice to on holidays—you keep the HNIC at bay by showing deference and respect. You do that because often all she wants is an acknowledgment from the young bloods that she exists and that, in some ways, she paved the way. The good thing about paying that respect, even if you're secretly rolling your eyes, is that you learn something. Like with the old aunt, you learn some history, some background, maybe even some genuine advice that helps make your experience easier. Any black person who has survived in a workplace for a period of time deserves our respect.

That leads to the next point, which is making sure that you don't walk in the door making assumptions based on how someone dresses or talks. While there are some people who make better allies than others, all of your fellow employees, particularly the other black ones, deserve a chance to show what they're made of before you jump to a conclusion.

Workplace Alliances

Marlena worked in a large Fortune 500 company as an auditor. An attractive black woman in her early 30s, she had worked in the company about five years when Crystal, another attractive sister, started working as an auditor fresh out of college. Crystal was very excited about her first job—a striver for sure.

Marlena (who was also a striver) worked from the assumption that since she was the "old head," the black person who had gotten to the company first and knew the ins and outs, Crystal should come up to Marlena first, introduce herself, pay the requisite respect, and ask Marlena for her hard-fought wisdom. That's the way Marlena was brought up by her parents, and she learned in church that you honor your elders, even if they are only about eight years older. Marlena thought Crystal was stuck up and wasn't about to make the first overture.

Crystal, on the other hand, had a different philosophy. She thought that when she came into a new job it was the elder's responsibility to welcome her, volunteer her knowledge, and make her path smoother, just as she planned to do for the brothers and sisters who came after her. Crystal thought Marlena was a snob.

For over a year, Marlena shrugged Crystal off like a bad habit while Crystal threw salt Marlena's way every chance she could. Each of them had built up such an attitude about the other in her own mind that one wouldn't so much as loan the other a subway token. The only reason they ever got to know each other and eventually ended up as friends was because Teresa, another young black woman hired a year after Crystal, made it her business to get to know every other black person in her department when she started. Eventually she let both Marlena and Crystal know that the other was a good, trustworthy person and that their snobby sister routines were only helping their supervisor to pit them against each other while screwing over them both.

Alliances are probably the most complex aspect of working. A friend of mine, who has a job as a supervisor, once called me complaining about how much people talk about non-work-related topics in the workplace. I pointed out to her that running your mouth at work was the social lubricant that kept the wheels of employment turning. She had to be reminded that her utter lack of socializing in past jobs was why she was the last to know about impending layoffs that affected her department and about upcoming key personnel changes that ended up causing her problems because she knew later rather than sooner. She eventually understood that while doing her job was her number one objective, it wouldn't kill her to spend five minutes here and there tripping over the company grapevine.

Whether you're a survivor, a striver, or a thriver, the game plan is the same—you have to go in remembering that you are not an island. Corny, but true. It doesn't matter if you're too shy to mutter a hello. You can't miss an opportunity to forge a valuable alliance while you work. It's not about using people, it's about allowing yourself to make your work experience as positive as you can. Ultimately, that is what you have to do as a black employee—create and build alliances, not expect them to already exist.

One of the first things you should do when you look for workplace alliances is view and evaluate the coworkers who do the job you are hired to do. If you are a secretary, get to know the other secretaries in your office—don't be so hung up on race that you fail to see that the person who you can have the best rapport with may be a white person old enough to be your mother or a Hispanic person young enough to be your son.

Bonding with another employee who does the same job doesn't mean you have to divulge your salary or share your personal secrets. It just means that you resist the tendency to pigeonhole people on first sight and make the assumption that you couldn't possibly have something in common with someone who is white, gay, of the opposite sex, or significantly older or younger than you.

Part of the difficulty in forming workplace alliances is that people have so many other considerations to juggle that it makes it hard to determine who to trust, how far that trust should go, and how everyone else might perceive a particular alliance.

As I said earlier, having an "old head," a person you can rely on in the workplace, can be helpful in making sure you attract and maintain healthy alliances. Ideally, all your workplace associates and friends can serve as mentors, each in his or her own way.

Challenging Friendships in the Workplace

Wendy, a black assembly-line worker, became good friends with Scott, a white assembly-line worker. They shared a love of old Western movies and Mexican food, and they were both from small towns. Wendy was happily married and was friends with many of the other black assembly-line workers, but because Scott was not only a man but a white one at that, Wendy dealt with her share of people making snide comments about her *boyfriend* or about them being *The Odd Couple*.

Wendy, however, wasn't going to let other people's opinions bother her. Scott was the only person who would take overtime shifts for her when she needed to take care of her sick child, he covered for her with their supervisor when she had problems working a certain piece of equipment, and they shared nothing more than simple friendship. Scott had her back, period, as much as some of her black coworkers and more than others.

Wendy had to face the fact that interracial relationships in the workplace, particularly with a member of the opposite sex, just draw more attention.

How does a black person handle opposite-sex friendships in the workplace? Although that is a tricky area in one respect with so much talk about sexual harassment, it really should not be handled much differently than making any other alliance.

It starts with not making assumptions about who people are. As a new employee, or as an employee trying to get to know a new employee, professional courtesy and friendliness are a good thing. Without jumping too quickly into shop talk or overly personal talk, let people reveal who they are. As I've said throughout this chapter, just listening without preconceived ideas will help you out more than anything.

When it comes to sexual innuendo, that's always out. Period. Regardless of the person's race, his or her position, how cool he or she seems with it, just keep the sexual jokes out of the workplace. If you do that, nobody will ever be able to say that a relationship with a coworker, let alone a subordinate or a boss, is out of line. These days, even compliments about somone's hair or clothes can have you wading into dangerous territory if you don't know the person really well.

This advice applies to women as well as men. When women start making too many jokes of a sexual nature, it's hard for a man to know when he has crossed the line when he makes one. Also, if a woman ever wants to make a complaint about offensive behavior or comments of a sexual nature, the last thing she needs is to have her employer show that she, too, is a dirty bird. One of the elements that courts look at in deciding whether a hostile sexual work environment exists is "welcomeness," which is if the accuser behaved in a way that might have signaled that she was not offended.

With men and women working side by side, I don't think making friendships with people of the opposite sex holds the same problems that it used to; but where it can be a 15 percent issue for a black employee is a situation where a white employee who is not used to dealing with blacks socially takes friendliness to be something more. Even in today's society, black men cannot

afford to be in positions where their actions look sexual or preda-
tory in nature around white women. Black men and white
women can be friends at work—and plenty are—but black men
should not take for granted that their friendship won't offend
someone at work if they don't read the smoke signals properly.

In addition to avoiding anything sexual, black employees
should be very observant about the way the rest of their coworkers do certain things and follow that lead. For example, if you
work in a place where everyone goes out to lunch in groups,
rather than in pairs, you will draw attention if you and an opposite-sex coworker always go out to lunch together. Even if nothing is going on, you risk the appearance that it is, or you risk your
coworker taking your behavior the wrong way with no one else
around to back you up. Granted, that can still happen if you work
in a place where employees do go to lunch in pairs, but it still
draws less attention if you're just rolling with the norm.

Alliances Between Black Men and Black Women

Roland was a black college student who had a summer
internship in a predominantly white office. Another black
intern, Lisa, had developed a dislike for Roland by the end of
the summer because he never went to lunch with her even
though he went to lunch with the other (white male) interns.
Later, when they were both hired, she found out from talking to another person in the office that Roland didn't go to
lunch with women, period, because he was afraid of someone assuming that he was interested in them romantically
or sexually.

While Roland's instincts may have been sound as an intern not wanting to make any false steps, his execution of this intent was greatly flawed. With the exception of some fields like construction work or nursing, where there is a disproportionate number of people of one sex doing the job, you are going to have to deal fairly equally with members of the opposite sex.

Avoidance is not a good tactic. For example, in the case of Roland, he had a lot in common with Lisa just by the two of them being the only black interns in a big company. While that did not mean they would necessarily bond, Roland never got the opportunity to know because he took the path of least resistance and left the door closed.

Hierarchical Relationships Between Black Employees

Another tricky aspect of building alliances is bonding with your black supervisor or subordinate. A lot of times the person with whom you have the most in common is another brother or sister who is your boss, or who you are the boss of. It can be done if the two of you keep it as a personal relationship that does not carry over into the workplace. One way you do that is by keeping those alliances to a minimum and keeping work out of personal conversation as much as possible when you do hang out. Also, do not rub in your personal relationship with others at work because that will just cause undue resentment from the white people who will question your objectivity.

Blacks and Formalized Unions

For some, unions are the one-size-fits-all way of choosing alliances. The existence of unions isn't as prevalent as it used to be, but in theory they have the right idea. People bond over the common tie of doing the same job or sharing the same craft, and they vow to stand together and protect each other's interests.

If you are a black person in the union, don't be a passive participant. Do more than pay your union dues—go to meetings, read the newsletter, run for office if you're a striver, and be a union steward if you're a thriver. Find whatever way works best for your personality to be active and involved so that your official brotherhood means something.

This advice—about being an active participant in widening your workplace alliances—holds true even if you do not belong to a union. If there are committees or task forces in your workplace, join them. Don't be afraid or intimidated or just plain disinterested because it appears that only the white employees get involved. My grandmother gave me that piece of advice a long time ago in the context of shopping and it holds even more true in the workplace—wherever you see all the white people go, that's where you at least want to visit to see what you may be missing.

To be a driver in the workplace (instead of instinctively operating from the survivor, striver, or thriver mind-set), it is important to honor the individuality of people. Developing workplace alliances isn't about using people, it's about thoughtfully befriending them for the purpose of making your work experience smoother and more positive. Part of thoughtfully befriending is to not instinctively classify an individual based on race, sex, or any other category. Otherwise, you may miss seeing who really has your back and who admires the surface of your back for the knife they'll eventually stick in it. Especially when it's a new environment, the best advice for sifting out alliances is just to lean back, listen, and learn.

7

FITTING IN WHILE STANDING OUT,
SETTLING IN
WITHOUT SELLING OUT

■

Frank, a black marketing analyst, didn't believe in attending company parties. He adamantly refused to go to any social event that did not take place during his normal work hours. He had a wife, four school-age children, aging parents with health problems; he was active in his church and college fraternity; and he was an avid bowler.

As long as he gave a hundred percent to his job, which he did when he was there, Frank didn't think it mattered or should matter whether he broke bread or hoisted a beer with his coworkers after work every now and then or attended the

company-sponsored get-togethers. He thought those parties
were for people trying to kiss ass or people who didn't have
a real life like he did. He also harbored the bias passed down
from his parents that it was never a good idea to give white
folks an opportunity to see him drink liquor or get too cozy
with him.

There is an old deodorant commercial that says that you don't
get a second chance to make a first impression. In the workplace,
especially when you're black, everything is an impression. Everything. You know it. I know it. Your bosses know it, even though
they'll never admit it.

First and foremost, though, you always have to keep your eye
on the ball. You can spend days on end concerned about how
white people perceive you, but you'll only drive yourself crazy.

Part of fitting in means doing your job well. Period. Never
slip up on the obvious. If the posted, expressed time for you to
be there is 7 A.M., then 7:30 is not an option. If you can't get up
that early, then find another job. At most jobs in America, your
7:30 is going to mysteriously be remembered as getting in an hour
late every day, while your white coworker who sashays in at 7:10
is going to be remembered as being mostly punctual. Depending
on where you work, your coming in even at 7:10 will be exam-
ined because of the assumption that the white employee has a
good reason, rather than being equally as derelict as yourself. It's
just an offshoot of what black parents have told their children
about having to get up earlier in the morning to compete. Today's

black parents should just tell their kids to get their butts up earlier to, at least, get to work on time.

In theory, Frank (from the example) has a point. If you're paid to do a job, why should it matter whether you attend a holiday party, a summer picnic, or even have a drink after work with your coworkers? Logically, it makes no sense additional time away from your family or your own interests should be required if you already give a lot to your job.

That is where knowing your workplace mentality comes in. If you're in it to win it, that is, if you're a striver, it should be a no-brainer that showing up at all company events, unless you have an incredibly good reason, is a must. (Actually, I think it is a must for all black employees, but your mode of operation will just determine how you do it.) Depending on the person and the job, showing up could be a quick visit, a leisurely meet-and-greet opportunity, or an in-your-face chance to show them what you're really made of.

In a nutshell, the reason we need to show up is so that we can demystify ourselves and be revealed as having the same red blood as every other human being on earth. It's an example of how we have to show the people we work with that 85 percent factor, where we are united in our motivation to come to work for the same reasons regardless of race.

I never cease to be amazed at how unaware many whites are about the diversity among black people. Once, when taking a white coworker to the black neighborhood where I grew up, she was astounded at how *normal* the people were dressed. She had assumed that the neighborhood folks would resemble something you would see on an old episode of *Starsky and Hutch*. (As I said in an earlier chapter, the blacks that many whites work with are actually their only contact with our world outside of what they see on television or the movies.)

On the other hand, it doesn't really matter what a fellow employee thinks of you, unless you think he is actually trying to do you harm. But managing workplace politics requires you to be as concerned about benign neglect or reckless disregard as much as you should be concerned about active, back-stabbing, direct malice.

Be a Driver in the Workplace

The concept of fitting in is practically synonymous with the concept of being a driver. That is, if you are a driver, then you make a conscious choice to fit in when you enter a particular workplace.

Just because you're a black employee does not mean you are going to have trouble fitting in to a predominantly white workplace. Because of your personality or the nature of the job you do, fitting in may be second nature. But when you walk into a new work situation, or the old one changes, the realization that you may need to do some adjusting to stay afloat is nothing more than pure driver mentality talking.

Instinctively, no one feels like she should have to change who she is. By choosing to be a driver, you're simply acknowledging that you are allowing yourself to shine in your best light. You're deciding to keep certain conversations out of the workplace. You're making the choice to keep certain interests to yourself. It's not about change, it's about making adjustments to reach your goal. A survivor's goal may be just not to draw undue attention. A striver's goal might be to draw the attention of the right bosses.

A thriver's goal may be not to stand out so much that it prevents him from doing his job properly.

So, what does this have to do with attending company parties and socializing with your coworkers? Easy: it's much harder to do harm to or create a bad experience for a friend than for a stranger. Overall, white people tend to think of friends in a much broader, more superficial spectrum than blacks. Black people have always used language to reflect our rich, ceaseless devotion to how we define and are connected to others in our life. A white person will typically refer to his friend, pal, or buddy. A black person, on the other hand, will talk about his blood, homey, ace, brother or sister, partner, cousin, my M.F., my nigga, and so on. Not only will we use variety in our names, we will be quick to correct others on the distinctions. "Frank is my running buddy, but Mike is my ace." "Teresa is my girl, but Carrie is like my sister."

As a communal group, I think blacks are clear about who knows our secrets, who knows our lies, and who knows nothing more than how much ice we like in our drinks. No matter what generation of blacks you look to, we've always had a thing about folks knowing our business. A long time ago, the black comic Marsha Warfield (who played the role of Roz the bailiff on *Night Court*), said black people couldn't play the game Trivial Pursuit because we only have three possible answers to every question and one is "Why you wanna know?"

Even our collective struggle as blacks and how we refer to ourselves—colored versus black versus African American—gets to our bottom-line issue of defining our relationship to other people. It's like the Yoruba proverb that says, "It's not what I'm called, it's what I answer to." But the truth is, it does matter what we're called. As author Toni Morrison said, "American means white, and Africanist people struggle to make the term applicable to themselves with ethnicity and hyphen after hyphen after hyphen."

If you can get a white coworker to call you "friend" at work, it makes it a lot more likely that the person will pause before stabbing you in the back. It also makes it more likely that the person will be your ally and a true comrade in the workplace. At the very least, your proximity might make you more alert to the presence of hot metal approaching your back. All whites are not your enemy, but, to the extent some are, as the saying goes, keep your friends close and your enemies closer. Or, as Oprah Winfrey has said, "Surround yourself with only people who are going to lift you higher."

Accepting people as individuals, without stereotyping, is the first step toward becoming their friend. If I think of you as someone who can be hurt by what I do or say, I'm going to be a lot less likely to make you an object of my harmful actions. Maybe it's just me, but if I think of someone as a friend, I'll guard his interest with almost as much care as I guard my own. On the other hand, if I don't think of someone as a friend, either because I actively dislike him or just don't consider him in my universe at all, then I'm indifferent about my words or actions where that person is concerned. I treasure my friends in the workplace. I don't expect them to scratch my back, I just expect them to let me know if there is a "Kick Me" sign taped to it.

From a practical standpoint, when someone files a discrimination lawsuit, one thing that happens in defense against the lawsuit is the investigation where we defense attorneys talk to everyone who worked with the plaintiff to see what's up. The more friends you have, the more people you will have to support your interpretation of events. (Never underestimate how a little loyalty will go a long way in that situation.)

Part of our reality as black employees is that we operate against the backdrop of a collective stereotype. That is, if you're black, you came from a poor, lower-class home, without a father or positive male role model, where you were exposed to drugs, poverty, excessive use of alcohol, and sex. You weren't exposed to the "nicer" things in life. That's the presumption until we say differently.

When you go to company picnics and holiday parties, bringing your husband, wife, significant other, relative, or friend is a way to make your experience as a black person count in a world where it just doesn't pay to be a statistic. It's one thing to know that Rufus is married. It's another thing to know that his wife's name is Susan and she seems mighty sweet and she likes to cook pound cake and whatever other details about his life that make Rufus a person easier to relate to. While you don't want to parade your straight-up dirt in the workplace, don't be afraid to sneak in enough of your outside life to show you as more than an ignorable black face.

In Frank's example from the beginning of this chapter, the one thing that Frank did do to personalize himself, and thus make him more approachable in the eyes of his coworkers and superiors, was to openly talk about his children and family. He brought in pictures, displayed his kids' artwork in his cubicle, and occasionally brought the children into work for brief visits. That, in part, made up for Frank's failure to show up at company-sponsored events, and that's why, when one of Frank's children came down with a serious illness, his company didn't hesitate to let him off for a few weeks with pay, send his family a huge fruit basket, and make it easy for him when he came back to work.

Considering that his company was too small to be covered by the Family and Medical Leave Act (FMLA), that was a generous gesture on his employer's part. (The FMLA requires companies of a certain size to offer a federally mandated leave of absence to employees who have personal health problems or close relatives with health problems. Along with the other conditions, such as the length of time allowed, the leave is not required to be paid. The point of the leave is to allow people to have a job to come back to if they have a personal or family health problem.)

My guess is that if Frank's white supervisors had not consistently seen how much fatherhood mattered to Frank, he would have been left taking time off for his child with no pay and having to worry about job security while he was gone. In some workplaces, he wouldn't have had the option of taking any time at all, because the assumption would have been that he was just trying to get a few extra days off.

Allowing your bosses to have a peek into your personal reality is no magic bullet against a truly racist boss. Handled carelessly, too much information (known by the younger set as "TMI") can be used as a weapon against you. It takes constantly evolving judgment to know what to share and what to keep on the down low about. For example, telling your bosses that you are stressed because of a close relative's health problem is probably a good thing. Telling them you can't decide whether to put yourself in rehab or just to try cutting back to four benders a week is something you might want to keep to yourself. Sharing with your bosses that you're going through a painful divorce might be a good thing. Telling them how you just caught your boyfriend in bed with your best friend the night before which is why you were two hours late for work after needing to be bailed out of jail is probably something you should keep to yourself. I think the trick to good judgment should be keeping your professionalism at the forefront of what you decide to share versus what you keep to yourself.

The best combination is to concentrate on doing a good job first and then sharing information about yourself that shows you are also a good person, and that sometimes your life as an employee can be influenced by your life outside of work. This is particularly true with your coworkers as well as your supervisors. Letting them know that you have a thing for NASCAR, that you like to play tennis on the weekends, or that you are planning on taking piano lessons makes it a little easier to fit in while staying true to yourself.

Deciding How Many of Your True Colors to Show

There are subtle ways that, as a black employee, you can be known and develop a more well-rounded relationship with your workplace. One of these is how you choose to show off in your environment.

With the exception of people who work in factories or out in the field (such as sales representatives), most employees have a workstation or a cubicle or an office to call their own at the place where they make their weekly bread. Every form of decoration or addition of detail tells your coworkers and your employer about your life and your interests, providing a peek into who you really are.

Again, part of letting yourself be known is just giving yourself an entry point for others—a place where you can meet at the common ground of 85 percent experiences. My point is not to make your environment white or white-centered, it's to make your environment right for you. For example, if you love baseball but your hero is Buck O'Neal from the Kansas City Monarchs, a member of the Negro Leagues, put up his poster or display his autographed baseball, regardless of whether you're a survivor, a striver, or a thriver. This might give a white colleague, who shares your interest in baseball, the opportunity to connect with you while learning something. On the other hand, a white colleague might surprise you by sharing your love of Buck O'Neal, thus, giving you another ally in the workplace.

A friend of mine frequently complains how he hates always having to "teach" white people—why is it that we have to constantly expose them to more about our world while we are expected to soak up every nuance of theirs. He's right. I get tired, too. The thing about other ethnic groups that we might not necessarily know much about, either, is that there is no expectation that we would know. For example, it's not expected to know about Chinese New Year or Cinco de Mayo but we better know about St. Patrick's Day.

With whites at work, it's supposed to be a given that we know all. The unspoken theme is: if it interests white America, it's interesting. But that's the price tag on choosing to interact in a space where people who look like me are not the ones running things. Sometimes I remind myself that the teaching comes from the doing, not the saying, anyway. (Remember, the proof is in the pudding, not the pudding mix.)

Besides, as black Americans, we can sometimes arrogantly think we are the only ones with things to teach. One of my favorite foods to eat is sushi. I learned to love it about eleven years ago when another reporter, a white guy originally from Seattle, invited me to lunch at a Japanese restaurant. The two of us may have lost touch, but my love for sushi remained. When I needed to learn about Alzheimer's disease recently, a white woman attorney (and true friend) passed on to me information about nursing homes and other places where I could find out more. Along the way, many of my white coworkers, as well as white subordinates and supervisors, have shared all kinds of information and support and knowledge when I've needed it, as well as when I didn't know I needed it. The real point here is that opening up the door in the first place allows it to then swing both ways. If I hang up a print by Jacob Lawrence in my office because I really like his art, a couple of my coworkers may develop an appreciation for his work. That's more important in the long run than the people who discount any art that is not white and European in origin. Building support and enough connection with people to stay in the loop is the true point.

A survivor's objective in the workplace when it comes to fitting in will be to avoid standing out as much as possible. Therefore, a survivor should and will go to all the company social events, express interest in the things that coworkers bring to her, and keep her personal life or viewpoints to a minimum for fear that something will be used against her. In terms of decoration, a survivor will stick to the safe things—plants, an old black-and-white wedding photo of her parents, a banner from her college, or a sporting souvenir from the local team. A survivor's goal in decoration is to have people feel comfortable when they are in the survivor's workspace, but not have anything excessively memorable.

On the other hand, a striver's objective will be very pinpointed and deliberate. A striver should figure out exactly what she is striving for and who, in particular, she needs to impress. If it is a particular position she wants, she has to remember that it is important for more than just the person in charge of giving the job to like her. She would be wise to attract the good graces of everyone who is affected by her getting that job. For example, if you work in an environment where people like to talk about the latest movies, bringing in some of your film memorabilia from home is a good idea. On the other hand, if you work in an environment filled with regular churchgoers, and the person handing out the type of promotion you want is a deacon of his congregation, you might want to keep that picture of you from the Wiccan induction ceremony at home.

A thriver has just as much reason to attend the company gatherings and pay attention to what his environment reflects as the survivor and the striver do. In marching to his own drumbeat, the thriver still needs to figure out what the rest of the orchestra is doing. Individuality is a thing of sparkling beauty, but unless you're a self-employed entrepreneur with no employees other than yourself, you've got to get into the rhythm of what others are thinking at the place where you collect that cash.

Black people know that the sister girl receptionist sitting by the elevator has the power to affect whether you'll see the official power behind the golden doors. We also know that the brother man custodian who cleans offices every night has the power to make sure that the private document that should have been shredded will *accidentally* make its way into your in-box. Again, that is why it is important to know your intention so that you are aware of all the players in the drama, not just the ones you think have lead roles.

Feeling in tune with the rhythm of your workplace means that you get along with people to make your work life as stress-free as you can, your home life as protected as you can, and your opportunity to move on to another gig as painless and easy as possible. As Ida B. Wells said, "Let the Afro-American depend on no party, but on himself, for his salvation. Let him continue toward education, character, and above all, put money in his purse."

■

I frequently wonder if we black people who have to work almost daily in the white work world are bilingual or just plain schizophrenic. One of the things I love about driving to work in the morning is that often it's the last contact I have with being submerged in my culture until the end of the day. I love listening to the radio and hearing the DJs joke about the latest thing our people are talking about. I look forward to hearing the latest jam from a soul singer before having to submerge myself into a world that's more about Shania Twain.

Like a Hispanic who speaks Spanish at home but doesn't mutter so much as a *gracias* while at work, we black people often feel like we're stepping in and out of parallel worlds. That's why many white bosses get a little nervous when they see more than two of us talking at work—usually our body language, our tone, our laughter reflect that we're dipping back into our comfort zone for a couple of minutes and that they are the ones who are irrelevant. They don't like that feeling.

Being true to your authentic self is the single most important thing you take into each experience. Work is no exception. In general, the concept of fitting in is not about squeezing yourself into a neat little two-dimensional screen that makes others feel more comfortable with you.

Ideally, if you've followed the other guidelines in the earlier part
of the book, fitting into the place you work is a natural thing.
That's because, if you've identified what motivates you and makes
you happy, and you've found a career or job that fulfills that goal,
then you've already done your research to find the right employer
in that field. Form good alliances once you get there, because fitting in is much smoother than being the outsider.

On the other hand, if done right, the flow can follow you.
The people in my former law firm, from the managing partner
to the file clerk, probably didn't quite picture an attorney in the
package of a dreadlock-wearing black woman who keeps crys-
tals on her desk, seriously refers to people's astrological charts,
and is comfortable with voicing the off-color comment that most
people have enough sense to keep in their heads. But I'd like to
think that I did fit in to the point of being missed when I left the
firm, because most of who I am just makes me a normal, 85 per-
center just like every other employee, with the rest being my pecu-
liar brand of flavor.

8

WHEN ATTITUDE IS THE ISSUE

■

Shanice's first annual evaluation was due. Patrick, her supervisor, told her that he wanted her to do a written self-evaluation and turn it in to him before she received his evaluation. Shanice had not been given the criteria she was to be judged by and she had never received a written set of goals to meet. All she received was a generic list of ratings ranging from 1 (unacceptable) to 5 (outstanding), so Shanice took a copy of her job description and wrote a point-by-point analysis of how she felt she had done her job that year. Shanice fairly and objectively, in her mind, ranked herself as either a 4 or 5 in each area, giving examples, but also listing ways she felt she could improve.

During the next staff meeting after she had turned in her self-evaluation, Patrick remarked to Shanice, in front of several of her coworkers, "You think pretty highly of yourself, don't you?" When Shanice sat down for her evaluation, he told her, "I haven't done your evaluation yet. I thought I'd give you an opportunity to redo yours before I did that."

This chapter begins our departure from focusing mostly on the 85 percent issues to issues where the 15 percent difference kicks in ferociously. This chapter addresses the "attitude" problem, also known as coming to work black. Since that sounds so negative, I have to explain it.

First of all, part of the problem with telling people that they have an attitude problem is that it is a subjective call. What you call attitude, I might call righteous indignation. What you call attitude, I might call frustration. What you call attitude, I might call personality.

While the interpretation of an attitude is subjective, when used in the hands of your employer, the issue of an employee's attitude is a mighty powerful tool. Saying that an employee has an attitude problem is one of those blanket terms just about everything can fall under. If you're late for work a couple of times a week, no matter how many times your supervisor scolds you, then you might be pegged with an attitude problem. If you roll your eyes every time your boss mentions the company retreat, you might be perceived as having an attitude problem. If you never volunteer for new projects while little Peggy Sue always sticks her hand up, you might be tagged with an attitude problem.

Every time your boss sticks that label on you, it's not necessarily wrong. Some people do have generally funky attitudes. You know them. So do I. They have a smart-ass answer for everything, or they are unnecessarily argumentative, or they have one relationship problem after another without appearing to learn any lessons.

Where attitude becomes an issue for a black person in the workplace, however, is when a black employee does not feel that his employer is doing right by him and he suspects it is because he is black, or at least suspects that it is based on some reason that is not fair. Before that employee gets to the point of filing a complaint, he usually develops an "attitude" to carry him through this rough work environment.

Ironically, my observation has been that it is usually the survivors and the strivers who develop an attitude when they perceive unfairness in the workplace. You see, I believe that thrivers have more of a built-in "attitude" throughout their work experience, which doesn't drastically change when they perceive a problem. It is survivors (who feel like they are just minding their own business) and strivers (who have been focused on advancement) who get thrown for a loop when things are not as they think they should be. Because neither of those personality types tend to buck the system anyway, they are more likely to demonstrate an "attitude" when they perceive anything smelly in the air.

Fighting a bad attitude and maintaining a good one can be the single most challenging area of your work life as a driver. When the situation starts to go sour, either because of the 85 percent issues that every one of your coworkers would complain about, or the 15 percent issues of "it's a black thang and you wouldn't understand," it becomes hard to drive yourself from underneath the covers without copping an attitude.

When you feel the attitude creeping into your system, or you know your anger and resentment are being perceived as attitude by your employer, that is when you have to become a driver. That is when you have to consciously snatch yourself by the back of the neck and figure out what's going on and come up with a game plan for how you're going to lick it. If you need to ask for a transfer, do it. If you need to start sending out resumes, do it. If you need to talk to someone you trust at your workplace who has the power to change things and who you don't think will burn you, do it.

When attitude becomes the issue for you as a black person, you've got to take action. Sometimes that action is with yourself, and sometimes it's with someone else. Sometimes the action is just to get the hell out of there.

One of the ways a black employee can guard against having an attitude that becomes a work problem is to accept that no matter how you work and how good you are, you may run across someone who feels differently about your performance for no reason other than your race.

Different Yardsticks

In the opening example, Shanice found herself smack dab up against that ever-changing yardstick that comes with some supervisors. You know, the yardstick that can create an attitude problem where there wasn't one before. The yardstick where white men are expected to project confidence and certainty about all things, to stand tall as pillars of strength and integrity, relied upon at all times and reliable in all circumstances. On the other hand, blacks, particularly black women, are supposed to be humble and self-effacing and ever knowledgeable about the opportunities they've been given (as opposed to earned) and grateful about the possibility that they'll be allowed to progress. While this is a sexist thing that all women can face, it's also a black thing.

A survivor probably would not have been in Shanice's position in the first place. For a survivor, the best way to handle this situation would be to significantly reduce her own self-evaluation. Even if a survivor thought she should have gotten a top-of-the-line evaluation, the survivor would have given herself ratings of three with an occasional sprinkling of four thrown in to allow the supervisor the luxury of either boosting the evaluation or reinforcing that the survivor probably wasn't as good as she wanted to be. The survivor's motivation would be not to rock the boat or put herself in any position that would cause her supervisor to increase the spotlight on her.

Now, in Shanice's situation, the striver probably would have seethed inwardly but redone the self-evaluation, bumping down her ratings according to how much she wanted to please the boss. The striver would have figured that Patrick would bump down the evaluation anyway, so this might be a way to work her way back into her boss's favor. Since a striver is motivated by getting ahead, the best strategy for her would have been to sit down with Patrick before changing the evaluation to get a real sense of Patrick's concern. Was it Shanice's overall high rating or some specific area that Patrick was concerned about? In doing so, Shanice would send the message to Patrick that she wanted to be fair to herself while addressing his concerns.

Depending on the temperament of a thriver, she would have either gone ballistic on Patrick then and there or done it on paper. Either way, the average thriver wouldn't change one word of that self-evaluation if she believed it when she wrote it. A thriver's motivation is usually to operate from internal integrity, even if the form of that integrity clashes with her superior's. Some thrivers would attempt to take the militant approach of making sure that they did not looked punked in the eyes of a white man. Other thrivers would just believe they were indeed that good.

What Shanice, who normally operates as a striver, did was to flip into full-throttle thriver mode. She told Patrick that she wrote what she believed, and that if he wanted to write an evaluation that reflected his differing opinion then he should do so. Shanice also made clear that she would provide a written response to his evaluation if she had any significant disagreements with it. The end result? Let's just say Shanice received an evaluation from Patrick that pretty closely resembled what she wrote about herself.

Shanice completely recognized that she took the chance that Patrick, as a form of revenge for her standing up for herself, could have written a very bad evaluation. What Shanice counted on was that he was going to stay in the neighborhood of fair, and in doing so would find himself having to write her a great evaluation. At the same time, Shanice affirmed that if he did not do so she was willing to go to the mat because it was ridiculous to expect her to lower her opinion about herself because Patrick had an issue with her confidence. For Shanice, while it would have been wonderful to have Patrick apologize, the reality is she knew it was gutsy to say as much as she did to him. In the end, she knew the bigger victory was having her evaluation accurately reflect her work accomplishments.

When I read this part of the book to a black male friend of mine, he raised this question: where do black men and white women fit in the workplace power hierarchy? Good question. Well, the answer is lower than white men, hence the reason why white women, black men, and black women (in that order, according to federal government statistics) make less money. Later that night I brought up the question at a party where there was a good mix of people to survey. My survey reinforced what I always thought—white men are at the top of the power hierarchy; black men have the double-edged sword of being men, which means they're expected to be bold and confident, but they're also black, so there better be a close correlation between what they say they can do and what they can actually do; white women have their own baggage—they've got the privilege of the right color, but the disadvantage of the wrong genitalia. As for black women, well, as a friend of mine (a white lesbian) once said, you're not considered dressed for success in the workplace unless you're wearing a white penis.

While my friend was right that looking and acting like the person who supervises you can help a lot, I don't believe you're screwed if you don't. If you go in thinking like that in every job, you will develop a premature attitude problem that will affect your self-esteem and your work.

Measuring Up

The one place white men and black men *can* bond is over sports. It's all out there—who can throw the ball higher, or harder, or with better precision is the purest, simplest kind of objective reality. White men can stand being bested at things that involve sheer physical prowess. It's no coincidence to me that white males can deal with black sports figures in a way that they can't seem to deal with black men in any other arena of their lives. My point is that, for example, a white male does not have to feel threatened that Michael Jordan can shoot a basket with more grace than it's ever been done. That can be written off as genetic, physical prowess. To the average sports-drenched male, athletes are

practically fictional characters; but let the casual (or real) evaluation process take place where white males sit around discussing
how others in the workplace do their jobs, and the objectivity
shifts to radical subjectivity with themselves being the standard.

A great example is the use of the word *token*. It's like the
phrase *affirmative action*. They are usually terms used by whites
to dismissively explain some positive job action that has happened
to a minority. "Jimmy was made vice president of marketing
because they needed a black token in the vice presidential ranks."
"Marcia got picked to second chair that trial because they just
needed a black to look good to the jury." "Beau was put in charge
of the night assembly line shift because of affirmative action, you
know."

It's amazing how little analysis whites do, especially white
males, when a white person gets a promotion or any kind of job
benefit. Competence is assumed, fairness is a given—lest you
point out that sharing the same skin tone as the decision maker
plays a part, you will quickly hear the catch-phrases "chip on your
shoulder" or "playing the race card."

On the other hand, when the script is flipped, not even a
whiff of unfairness can be allowed if a white employee is on the
losing end. As an employment defense attorney, the running joke
at the firms I've worked at is that the plaintiff in an age discrimination case is probably a white male. You see, in a federal age
discrimination case, a person over the age of 40 years old can file
a claim if he believes he's suffered adverse employment action in
favor of someone under the age of 40. One of my favorite things
to say is, "I wish I had until the age of 40 before I suffered from
discrimination, I'd still have a few more good years left."

Because I am a black woman who has done plaintiff work
(and has personally dealt with bouts of discrimination in my own

life and the lives of my loved ones), I'm usually one of the few employment defense attorneys who can detect the kernel of truth in what a plaintiff claims, even in some of the more outrageous lawsuits.

What whites often don't realize is that hearing demeaning, dismissive comments over the years, about "tokens" and "affirmative action" can take its toll. Some people have those wonderful personalities that can deflect that kind of negativity. Most of us have to build defenses to deal with it. Unfortunately, part of those defenses can come across as if you are carrying a boulder (rather than a chip) on your shoulder.

All Kinds of Ignorance

A lot of the perceived attitude problem isn't about the black employee at all; it's about the person who is doing the perceiving. Truth is, whites are not always very good at reading the moods or facial expressions of black people. It never ceases to amaze me that the frame of reference many white Americans have for blacks comes from watching *Good Times* or *The Jeffersons* on television. Aside from having to know white people inside out, blacks folks aren't much better at knowing much actual, factual information about other ethnic groups. Many of us only know about Hispanics from watching *Chico and the Man*, and many of us don't know anything about Native Americans other than claiming that we've got some Native American blood, which is why we have "good hair."

Blacks, on the other hand, can't afford to enter the work force with the same level of ignorance about white America that whites can have for every other minority group.

In the past year alone, I've had to explain to my white coworkers, at different times, who Lauren Hill, Luther Vandross, and P. Diddy were. Can you imagine me going to work and having to say that I had never heard of Gwyneth Paltrow, Garth Brooks, or Richard Simmons? They would look at me with disbelief, amazed at how I managed to make it to a professional career in such cultural ignorance. They would say Gwyneth and Garth and Richard were "mainstream," and how could I pick up a newspaper or magazine or watch television without hearing of them? Didn't I see *Shakespeare in Love*, or Garth's NBC special, or Richard's *Oldies but Goodies* tape on the shopping network? Yet, I've encountered white coworkers my age who have never heard of *Jet* magazine, don't know that Luther's *Never Too Much* is a classic, and don't remember P. Diddy from when he was sampling as Puff Daddy.

I once saw a grown woman on *Who Wants to Be a Millionaire* blank on the question, "Who is the 'Queen of Soul'?" I remember asking how any game show contestant over the age of 30 could not know that Aretha Franklin is the Queen of Soul. I'll admit, a lot of white folks probably scratched their head at that one, too.

Granted, my 74-year-old grandmother might not know many of these black references either, but then my grandmother hasn't been a member of the workforce for about 20 years and isn't expected to know what's near and dear to white folks' hearts. Cliffie, my grandmother, had to ask me in the summer of 2000 with a note of exasperation in her voice, who exactly this "Harry Potter" was and why did everyone on television keep mentioning him when they spoke.

All of us are ignorant of others. Period. No matter how many seminars or workshops or mandatory training sessions we go to, there's only so much any of us know or can be expected to know about someone who has a different frame of reference than we do. A few months ago, a male coworker and I were leaving a restaurant. I was responding to something he said while walking and then realized that he wasn't beside me any more. I looked back and he was helping a mother get her stroller through the door. We both saw the woman at the same time and I didn't even stop to think about helping her. Never crossed my mind. I have no kids and have never struggled with a stroller in my life. My friend, however, has three kids, one a toddler, so he instinctively identified with the woman, her problem, and the solution. Race and culture are a lot like that. As a society we're trained to be more culturally sensitive, but here's the bottom line: you can't teach instinctive cultural awareness.

The level of ignorance allowed by whites in the workplace is one of the reasons why a lot of black employees have an attitude problem. Not every black person believes that every white person is ignorant, but blacks can be resentful that this ignorance can be so open and blatant.

When the majority of the people you work with don't know the names of the top pop culture figures with your skin color (unless the person has gone completely mainstream), it takes its toll on you. For most blacks this is an example of how whites don't have any interest in knowing anything about blacks unless it directly benefits them.

During a diversity committee meeting for a newspaper I worked at, the topic was what things we needed to emphasize in order to recruit more black journalists. After hearing a whole lot of talk about the outlets for entertainment and the number of blacks who already worked at the paper, I had to ask the editors, "What do you use to attract nonminority candidates to apply?" One editor replied, "Oh, well, the great school system, the arts community, the fabulous housing market, and the beautiful weather." One of the blacks in the group promptly piped up, "Well, black people have kids, and like the arts, and like good weather, and have to have some place to live, so maybe we should mention that."

Black in Charge

In general, many whites (white supervisors in particular) have never had to deal with black people before entering the workplace. What took me by surprise in law school was the number of people who have never had to deal with a black person in authority—not a relative, teacher, family friend, minister, or police officer—not one person of color to hold power firmly over their head. I could tell by the complete and utter contempt a handful of my classmates exhibited whenever one of the two black professors *dared* to call on them in class. While I mention this one example, I've had many whites express that they didn't deal with a "live" black person for the first time until they were an adult. While blacks have broken many barriers, statistically speaking, my point isn't a reach. For example, if blacks comprise only 11 percent of the workforce and of these, only 18 percent of black men hold managerial or white-collar jobs, it's fair to say that many whites might go a long time before encountering a black occupying a position of authority. I remember one white coworker sharing with me his surprise at encountering so many black professionals when taking a business trip to Detroit. Coincidentally, another white coworker explained to me how she didn't like the movie *Boomerang* because she felt it was unrealistic that everyone who worked at the company in the movie was black. She said she liked it better and found movies more realistic when whites were more prominently featured. Such a division would more accurately reflect the environment that she grew up in and was familiar with.

I came to understand that with power and authority comes fear, and with certain kinds of fear comes respect. Notice I said *certain kinds* of fear. If I fear you're going to steal my purse or rape my sister, then I'm not going to respect you, but if I fear that you have the power to flunk me, fire me, punish me, or otherwise alter my life, then subconsciously I'm going to have a healthy respect for your ability to change my reality.

If you've been taught that a certain group of people are not deserving of power *and* you never see a member of that group wielding that kind of power, then it is harder for you to respect members of that group—not just as bosses, but as peers and even as subordinates. The effect of this on blacks is a heavy, pervasive feeling of never being good enough no matter what you do—a feeling that, for many black employees, blossoms into resentment and anger.

A favorite quote of mine from author James Baldwin is "Not everything that is faced can be changed, but nothing can be changed until it is faced."

How do survivors deal with this attitude problem? They usually don't deal with it much at all. Attitude is not an issue for survivors. They are the black employees who go to work and keep their eyes on the prize, so to speak. Survivors appreciate having a job in the first place and remember that every job has problems.

Strivers only start getting an attitude when they get so beaten down by the prevailing system, they have no alternative but to develop a 'tude. The two professions I've been in—journalism and law—both have strong black national professional organizations, with local chapters in larger cities. I've seen many black strivers—too busy to come to meetings when succeeding because they thought the group was a little too militant—suddenly become poster children for civil rights the second they personally get screwed over.

As I wrote earlier, thrivers are usually slow to develop the "attitude problem" because they usually come in the door with a personality that lets their employers know that they see the world differently. As thrivers get older that works more to their benefit, because employees get less reactionary when an older black thriver speaks his mind. However, when a thriver believes problems have gone completely over the top, he might be just the one who waltzes over to the EEOC (Equal Employment Opportunity Commission) office to file a complaint. Mentally, it is a short leap from not being a company guy or girl to being a non-company guy or girl who sues.

Think White, Think Right?

Another place where strivers (not to mention survivors and thrivers) can find themselves dealing with the slap of cultural clash is on the issue of judgment. Bad judgment is the first cousin to the attitude problem.

The exercise of good judgment is an implicit part of any job you do. It is also the collective umbrella of subjectivity that probably most drives black folks crazy in the workplace. Often, judgment is nothing more than comparing how I would have done something to how you would have done something, and if you're the boss your judgment trumps mine.

Jessica was a full-blown striver who worked as an accountant. Jessica had a great education and was ambitious, smart, and pretty, with a very likeable, laid-back personality. One day she got a nasty e-mail message from a client while she was out to lunch. The client, an East Coast white man, didn't like the way Jessica had communicated an issue about his account. Jessica didn't appreciate the tart tone of the client's e-mail, so she forwarded it to her boss, Frank (who is white), suggesting that he talk to the client and smooth his ruffled feathers since she was offended by the man's comments and thought it more appropriate that Frank deal with him. Several weeks later, when Jessica was having issues with Frank on an unrelated matter, he brought up her "bad judgment" in how she had handled the client's complaints. Frank was of the opinion that she should have called the client immediately and apologized.

Jessica, on the other hand, was blown away by the fact that her judgment was criticized, figuring that if she had called the client that day with any inkling of a tone in her voice, then she would have been called on the carpet. More important, as a black woman, Jessica felt that in no way, shape, or form had her firm empowered her to take it upon herself to make a bold move like that with a client who was already angry. Frank's insistence that, in her place, he would have done that sounded to Jessica like an Olympic athlete with a gold medal in swimming telling a person on crutches that he should have jumped into a pool to save a drowning child.

Power. Empowerment. Lack of power. Powerlessness. Those are the issues that dictate the attitude you have as a black person when you go to work in the morning, if you let them overwhelm you.

By the time Jessica was done talking to Frank, damn right she had an attitude. She had the attitude that she was tired of being on the bottom of the totem pole, below everyone else at this particular job (including the brothers) and of being given the black woman workload of low-sizzle assignments and marginal involvement. The combination of being both black and a woman intensifies the issue—remember, black women make less on the average than everyone else, including black men. When a problem came up, was she supposed to put on her superhero suit and operate like Batman or Superman, when she was neither white nor in possession of a cape?

So, what were Jessica's options?

First of all, Jessica's initial instinct was a good one. Handling this fool of a client required thought and finesse. That's why she had to figure out her objective. Sometimes what happens with us black folks is that we confuse validating our instincts with meeting our objective. In other words, we need to worry less about being fronted and more about covering our butts. The automatic degree that every black person should have at work—to cover both 85 percent issues and 15 percent issues—is a C.Y.A. (Cover Your Ass). The theme of this book, in a nutshell, is that as a black employee you stand out, whether you're a survivor, a striver, or a thriver; therefore, to be a driver, covering your butt is even more important because a black backside is easier to pick out of a lineup.

That's where the motivations of the survivor versus the striver versus the thriver come into play. A survivor would probably be mortified that this was a problem at all. A survivor's motivation would be to make sure that the boss didn't find out about this unless absolutely necessary, so the survivor probably would pick up the phone immediately, hunt the client down, and play nice-nice until she was certain that everything was smoothed over. Then the survivor would mention the incident in a very minimized or incidental way to her boss, on the off-chance the client mentioned it in passing.

The striver, in his or her motivation to get ahead, would take the approach of hunting down the boss immediately to explain the situation; but a true striver would have a plan of action in full effect first. The striver would not hunt down the boss just to whine or vent but to propose a specific approach to the problem. The striver brother or sister would also make clear to the boss that it was the boss's decision to make.

A thriver would handle it depending on just how pissed off she was, and whether this was a last-straw or out-of-the-blue situation. If it was a last-straw situation, where the thriver brother or sister had been tired of dealing with the client's attitude for a while anyway, then the thriver would probably fire off a response by e-mail, or directly if he or she could reach the client, and call it a day. He or she would not knock him- or herself out telling the boss, figuring that the client's diatribe was a personal problem and not something that the boss needed to be bothered with anyway.

Each of these types would have handled it based on his or her inherent motivations: the survivor in an effort to not be blamed for any negative fallout, the striver to not have this incident affect his or her goals to get ahead, and the thriver to not let him or herself be treated badly for any reason.

Respect Is More than an Aretha Tune

Another reason why blacks have to deal with the "attitude" problem is that culturally, we generally place a higher premium on being respected than whites do. I consider it an offshoot of living in a society where the word *nigger* was an agreed-upon way of addressing black folks, and black men were supposed to be OK with the fact that they could openly be called "boy."

Lenora had a job as a communications specialist in her department. Richard was the only other person in the department who held the same title. When it was time to decide who was up for a review, the supervisor told Richard that everyone with his title was exempt from a review that year. The only problem with that decision was that the supervisor had scheduled Lenora for a review in the upcoming week. When Lenora questioned the decision, her boss hemmed and hawed on why Richard was exempt from a review and she wasn't. In the end, he ended up giving both of them a review, which just fueled Lenora's suspicions that she was unfairly receiving harsher treatment. Lenora's boss later wondered why she had an attitude problem.

Lenora was a thriver. That's why she called her boss on his blatant discrepancy. Because Lenora had strong self-esteem, she didn't assume that her boss was trying to say that she needed to be criticized about her work and Richard didn't.

Unfortunately, the so-called attitude problem that we black folks get saddled with is a defense mechanism to keep ourselves from internalizing the ways we perceive ourselves being treated. Attitude sometimes exists as the only way for black people to express our discontent with our employers, as opposed to out-and-out insurrection.

One way that blacks express their attitude problem is by operating on the infamous "colored people" (C.P.) time. While our chronic lateness is in great part a cultural issue, in the workplace it can be a passive-aggressive way to express our attitude toward our employer.

In the end, the power structure of the workplace is why the attitude issue rears its ugly head in the first place. Sometimes it results from the frustrations of dealing with institutionalized racism, and sometimes it is just a perception on the part of whites regarding any negative display of emotion on a black person's part. Aside from when it manifests itself in an objective fashion, a lot of blacks just get tired of being graded at work on how we make the white folks in the room feel. Ultimately, that's what the attitude problem is about. It's about feeling as if we are judged disproportionately by the reactions we inspire in others. In other words, you feel threatened, so I appear to be angry. You feel nervous, so I appear to be sullen. You feel intimidated, so I appear to be icy.

Despite all our good reasons for indulging in a bad attitude in the workplace, we can never let that attitude crush us. Sometimes it will show. Life is going bad at home, you've got money problems, health problems, marriage problems, or kid problems, and the last thing you want to hear is your boss heaping another problem on your plate as you see him throw loving accolades to your white coworkers. But showing your anger, frustration, fear, or hurt is *not* an option 99 times out of 100. Do not let your attitude ruin your experience. At the very least don't let it show, because once you do, you become your attitude and your attitude starts to define your experience.

No matter how hard it is, no matter how many reasons you have not to, never go to work with a demeanor that expresses anything short of "I'm glad to be here and you should be damn glad to have me." With that attitude, you can roll through whatever comes up.

9

LAW AND ORDER, OR WHAT TO DO IF YOU DECIDE TO SUE

■

> Malik was a fast-food worker at the local food court in a small town with a thriving casino industry. One day while he was working with Patty, his overweight white coworker, Patty criticized something Malik was doing. He responded by saying, "Stay out of my business, Nanook, you killer whale." Patty shot back, "At least I don't look like a black monkey hanging out at the zoo." Phyllis, another white coworker, overheard this and laughed. For the next few months, Patty and Phyllis teased Malik and referred to him as "Monkey Boy."

As I said at the end of the last chapter, attitude rules. No matter what kind of attitude others try to assign to you, you should go to work with your head held high and proud to be a working black, but for some people there comes a day when they've got to take their attitude to another level. There are times when, whether survivor, striver, or thriver, that 15 percent difference becomes your entire work experience and you can't take it anymore.

To Sue or Not to Sue

In the example above, you've got to wonder if Malik had the basis for a lawsuit. Depends. Many questions have to be asked. How many employees does Malik's employer have? Under state and federal law employers cannot be sued for discrimination unless they employ over a certain number of employees. Was this the first time Malik was teased about his race? Did he laugh or join in when he was teased, or did he tell the teasers he found the comments offensive? Does his workplace have a policy regarding complaints? Did Malik complain according to the policy? If Malik hasn't complained, does his employer even know about the racial teasing? What does Malik want? Does he want the teasing to stop, or does he simply want an apology? Does he want Patty and Phyllis fired? Is Malik just after money and, if so, how much does he want? How much could he get?

As Whitney Sings, "How Will I Know?"

Deciding whether you should bring a lawsuit against your employer is one of the single most important decisions you'll ever make. You can't take it lightly because, as my employment law

professor said, if you bring a lawsuit against your employer, sometimes even when you win, you lose. His point was that while you
may have the law and the facts on your side (or at least on your
side enough to convince a jury that you're in the right), you've
put a nice little red and white target squarely on your back for
your next employer. Not to mention the protracted stress you
inevitably put yourself and your family under to get that mythi-
cal, beloved jury verdict in your hands.

Here's the funny part. Most people sue because, at some
level, they want the world to know that their boss is a racist, bigoted jerk. They also want to be vindicated for every indignity
they believe they suffered and show everyone that they are heroic
for helping prevent this from happening to anyone ever again. At
the very least, the less altruistic blacks who sue figure that everyone deserves to know how much cash they were able to milk from
the bloodsuckers who screwed them over.

But most lawsuits are settled out of court. This means that
no one is going to know anything about how wrong your
employer was, because 99 percent of the time you and your
employer will sign a confidentiality agreement, stating that you
can't tell anyone about the settlement *and* that the settlement isn't
an admission of guilt on the part of the employer. More important, many confidentiality agreements have what is called a "liq-
uidated damages" clause, which means that you can be taken to
court and essentially fined a set amount of money for each time
it can be proved that you spoke about the agreement. These
amounts can be anywhere from $1,000 per instance on up,
depending on the size of the settlement and how big a badass
your employer or former employer wants to be. That's one sure
way to convince people to keep their mouths shut, and companies know it.

That's why it is really important to sit down and examine what your intent is in making a complaint and the best way to get that complaint heard. If you want it to be official, put it in writing to your immediate supervisor and copy the people above him or her. If your company has an internal grievance procedure, follow that to the letter with no personalized variations. If you work in a more informal environment, ask your boss to lunch and try that approach.

How you start is how you finish. If you're going to be a driving force in taking the lawsuit avenue, date and document everything, and if it is possible, always think in terms of problem resolution rather than revenge or getting even. You always look better when you take the high road, and if you ever do find yourself in front of a judge and jury, the side whose case looks better is usually the side with the better chance of winning.

Why Some People Seek Legal Advice

When things are going badly at work, you feel as if someone has pushed you into a corner and is building piles and piles of wet sand that you can't climb over, can't see under, and can't breathe through. You know that if you don't get out before the last pile of sand has been built in front of you, you'll die of suffocation if you don't perish from hopelessness first.

At some point, it all merges together—fear, hopelessness, anger, depression, and apathy. You get to the point where you can't think about your job situation, you can only feel the heaviness of it. Thinking rationally about your job, your pay, the place you work, and the people you work with becomes harder than lifting weights at the gym, and when even one other black coworker shares your pain, feels that strain of despair, you have confirmation in your heart and in your head that you're being screwed and the only question is what to do about it.

That's where suing comes in.

When it feels that bad, that unfair, that just plain ol' wrong, you go right to the place that says, "Sue the bastards, sue the bastards for everything they have, and make them feel this same pain." But taking that step requires you to know that the ground ahead could be quicksand rather than sweet, firm earth.

Marissa worked at her company as a mail handler. She started off in the mailroom at the age of 18 and was still at the same job in the mailroom approximately one college degree and eleven years later. Because she was ready to start making more money, and despite the fact that her job in the mailroom was super easy, she decided to apply for other jobs in the company. She felt, with her degree and years of service, that the company owed a black woman the chance to climb the ladder.

The company found it easier to give bright new college graduates a job in middle management than to give a higher-level job to someone who was, at best, a mediocre mail handler. After getting passed over for one too many jobs, Marissa filed an EEOC complaint for race and sex discrimination. Then she hired an attorney and filed a lawsuit. The case eventually went to trial. Marissa won in a jury trial and was awarded $23,000 in actual damages and $3.5 million in punitive damages. Her company appealed and won, with the appeal going all the way up the circuit. The court reduced her award of damages to $43,000, half of which she had to give to her attorneys in fees and expenses.

From the day Marissa filed her EEOC complaint to the day she walked out of her attorney's office with less than $20,000 was approximately four and a half years. And, oh yeah, she still worked for the company as a mail handler.

When it comes to pursuing legal remedies in your job, it's necessary for you to be the most careful driver of all. Complaints, especially ones that may lead to litigation, are not tactics to be taken lightly. You don't get to pick and choose how people will react, and, regardless of how many laws there are forbidding retaliation, paycheck signers will not appreciate a lawsuit while you still work there. Supervisors will act nervous, and coworkers may suddenly act weird around you for fear they'll be called as a witness or dragged into the lawsuit somehow. So you have to ask yourself what you're driving yourself to achieve. Vindication? Peace of mind? Money? To be heard?

The destination decides the route. For example, if the destination is simply to be heard, to alert your employer to a problem, then you can sit down with your supervisor or with someone in human resources. Note that while the law protects you against negative employment action arising from your complaint (legal retaliation), it doesn't protect you from someone feeling annoyed, resentful, or defensive; do not sit down and take that route if you're the kind of person who lacks the ability to deal with contention.

If you feel that your problem is one of those 85 percent issues—workers' compensation or the Family and Medical Leave Act, for example—that is when you need to go talk to someone in human resources to get your questions answered. When it comes to one of those color-free issues, you're always better off getting your information right from the horse's mouth rather than assuming that there will be racial implications.

If you feel that what has been done to you is based on race and you find it particularly egregious, go for broke and file an EEOC complaint. Again, you've got to ask yourself what that will net you, after the time and energy you will have to give to that process. When you do feel driven to that point, the hardest thing to understand is that no one is ever going to apologize to you for his/her discrimination or racism. Doesn't happen. Therefore, if you're trying to get yourself a winning jury verdict, know that it never comes with a "You were right, I was wrong, and I'm sorry" attached.

There's Law but Not Always Order

Real-life litigation is not like the movies or television. Fake drama gives you no indication of just how time-consuming, grueling, and emotionally taxing suing your employer can be. It's amazing how many employment laws exist. There's the Family and Medical Leave Act (FMLA). There's the Americans with Disabilities Act (ADA). There's workers' compensation. There's state law. There's local law. There's a whole bunch of laws out there. When it comes to racial discrimination, the federal law primarily used is Title VII, which came about as part of the Civil Rights Act of 1964. Title VII prohibits job discrimination against employees on

the basis of race, color, national origin, religion, and gender at any
stage of the employment process. But there are a range of other
laws and remedies that can also affect you as a black person—
gender, age, pregnancy, retaliation, and more.

Back to Marissa. She got the satisfaction of taking her case
to trial. She got the emotional payoff of having a jury find in her
favor, with millions of dollars added in punitive damages to make
it really hit home.

But what Marissa learned along the way is that when David
meets Goliath, it's more like David meets Hotshot, Superior, and
Paid LLP, Goliath's litigation team, who bills by the hour and has
an arsenal of pistols, cannons, and smoke bombs at their disposal
to counteract David's lonely, overworked slingshot.

Sometimes the slingshot can beat the army of weapons. Ask
Exxon, Coca-Cola, Adams' Mark, Denny's, and other big companies that have suffered embarrassing and huge losses when
employment discrimination claims were brought against them.
But a single employee, hiring a solo attorney or an attorney for
a small firm (because the big firms almost always represent the
employers), needs to have hardy stamina to fight the good fight.

Peter worked in a big corporation in the Midwest for several
years. At the time that he decided to sue his company for race
discrimination, he had a condominium and two cars. One
day, out of the clear blue sky, Peter was fired. He believed the
only reason was because he was black. Even though he was
able to find another good job in the same industry, he decided
to file an EEOC complaint for the purpose of punishing his for-

mer employer. As a pride-filled black man, he felt he had no other choice. Peter looked for an attorney after he got the right-to-sue letter required by law, but none thought he had a good enough case. (A right-to-sue letter is a legal document that the EEOC is required to provide before a potential plaintiff is allowed to file a lawsuit.) Peter stubbornly refused to believe that and filed the lawsuit himself as a *pro se* plaintiff. (In legal jargon, *pro se* meant that he was representing himself, and every expense had to come out of his own pocket instead of being fronted by an attorney.) Peter was so serious and determined to not give up this lawsuit that even when his former employer offered to settle with him, he said no. He lost his new job because of the time it took to research his own case and respond to every motion from the other side. Peter also lost his condo, both of his cars, and his credit rating because he had to drain his savings and his 401K for depositions and other expenses. The last time I talked to Peter a few years ago, he was enrolled in law school out-of-state and still fighting Goliath Inc.

There is no one-size-fits-all method for determining whether to pursue a claim for discrimination. Every person's set of facts is different and laced with just enough nuance to separate it from similar cases.

Peter was a striver who decided to become a full-bodied thriver. Something about what his boss did to him and the reasons given struck him to the core of his being and he wasn't willing to let it go, no matter how much he had to lose in order to win. Even when the company was willing to settle with him for a decent amount, Peter found it better to risk getting nothing than to get something and have to keep his mouth shut about it. It was a big leap for a former company man who had his eye on moving up the corporate ladder as a striver to become the chief antagonist in open warfare. A black survivor wouldn't have risked a damn thing to prove a point—let alone a sweet condo and two nice cars—and the average striver would have walked away with the settlement (and the signed confidentiality agreement) ready to make his or her mark somewhere else.

Ultimately, the final decision of how much he was willing to lose was all on Peter. For Peter, being a driver meant giving up everything he owned so he wouldn't feel as if he had rolled over for mere money. Another black person might have taken the initial settlement offer made by the company, feeling that he might as well take the money because it couldn't change what had already happened.

Which is another point that people don't realize. When an employee brings a discrimination suit after he or she has been fired from the job, reinstatement is rarely a court-ordered option.

Legal Discrimination in a Nutshell

I should start off by saying that discrimination in and of itself is not wrong or unlawful. *Discrimination* just means "to distinguish." When you buy a red sweater instead of a purple one, you're using your power of discrimination to make a choice. When you decide to apply for Job A instead of Job B because Job A pays more than what you are making and Job B doesn't, you are discriminating between two possibilities. When an employer hires me because I'm a University of Kansas graduate and he is a Jayhawks fan instead of hiring a candidate who is a Kansas State Wildcat, hey, I have to applaud the employer's good taste and discrimination.

The law doesn't say that employers can't discriminate, the law just maintains that an employer cannot unlawfully discriminate. Usually the difference rests on the basis of why the person is discriminating (or choosing) between one person or one course of action and another.

The basics start with the law. Almost every state has antidiscrimination laws, which prohibit adverse employment actions on the basis of race or other specific areas of protection. Being in a protected class means that you are able to claim legal discrimination based on your membership in that class. The groups that federal laws generally protect are distinguished by race, creed, color, sex, disability, pregnancy, veteran status, and age. I was stunned to discover that not every state prohibits discrimination on the basis of race. I worked on a case once that required me to put in a clause about Alabama state law prohibiting race discrimination. After looking in all the obvious places to find what I thought was a basic fact, I made a call to the Alabama counsel and found that there was no state law. There was a state law prohibiting discrimination on the basis of age, but not race. Hmmmmm.

If you receive an adverse employment action because of your membership in a "protected class," according to Congress, that is illegal. For example, if your boss passes you up for a promotion because you are black, you have received an adverse employment action (being passed over for a promotion) based on your membership in a class (race) the law protects. Now if you want to bring a federal lawsuit for employment discrimination, stating that your boss didn't give you a job because you mentioned in your interview that you're a Yankees fan and your boss likes the Mets, well, you're out of luck, because the law doesn't make sports fans a protected class.

Basically, the employment relationship is governed by the at-will concept. That means that, unless you work under a contract or in a union, you work at the will of your employer. In plain English, you can quit any time you want and your employer can kick you to the curb any time she wants as long as she isn't firing you for one of the narrowly stated reasons recognized by the law. Although most employment is *at will*, if you're an executive or a professional in an industry that typically uses employment contracts, you many not be an at-will employee after all. In this case, you need to remember that your contract will govern the bounds of your employment relationship. The key thing to note is that just because something is in writing doesn't mean you're working under a contract. For example, a prospective employer writing a letter offering you a job does not automatically mean that you are under a contract. In fact, it usually doesn't mean that at all, and an employer with a good lawyer will make sure the offer explicitly states that the letter is not a contract and that you're an at-will employee who can be terminated without cause.

Once you get the job, however, if your boss is making your life a living hell, that doesn't mean the court will offer you protection. If we're talking about race rather than other forms of legally protected discrimination, then you only have a case if your boss is making your life a living hell because of your race.

That is one of the reasons why there is no such thing as reverse discrimination when discrimination refers to whites. While the federal law prohibiting discrimination may have come about because of black Americans, you know a 1960-something

Congress was going to make sure that the umbrella included everyone, including white folks. (Not to mention that little "equal protection" thing in constitutional law.) So, if a black supervisor keeps passing over the white men in a department because they are white and male, one or all of those men who have been passed over for a job can bring a race and gender discrimination lawsuit. The law doesn't recognize the concept *reverse* discrimination, it only recognizes discrimination.

Employment discrimination is a complex area of law that applies to a number of different scenarios. In general, Title VII is the primary federal law that governs employment discrimination, and most state laws governing racial discrimination use Title VII as the guideline. Title VII covers private employers, federal, state, and local governments, and educational institutions that employ 15 or more individuals.

Basically, any employee or job applicant who believes that he or she has been discriminated against in regard to hiring, firing, compensation, assignment, transfer, promotion, layoff, job advertisement, recruitment, benefits, or any other terms or conditions of employment has a *prima facie* case. *Prima facie* is just legal talk that means you have the right to put the needle on the record and start the song.

Other areas of discrimination where a black employee could bring a federal discrimination claim on the basis of race include harassment (also known as "hostile work environment"), and retaliation against an employee for filing a charge of discrimination, participating in an investigation, or opposing discriminatory practices.

One of the reasons why you should consult an attorney before deciding to take any action against your employer is that the words *discrimination*, *harassment*, and *retaliation* have common everyday meanings separate and apart from their legal meanings.

When I was a solo practitioner as a plaintiff's attorney, I would frequently get calls from black employees saying that their boss was harassing them and they wanted to know if they could file a lawsuit. Often, what they would call harassment would be things such as their boss telling them that they needed to be at work on time, or criticizing how they did their job, or asking them questions that they thought were none of their boss's business. People didn't want to hear that conduct can be harassing, but the law only protects you if the harassment is based on your membership in a protected class.

Your boss can make fun of the fact that you think that mixing plaids and stripes in the same outfit is good fashion sense when you work as a computer programmer. You can feel like she is harassing you because she doesn't say hello to you in the morning with the same enthusiasm she speaks to your white coworkers, or because she doesn't like that you use smiley faces when you send e-mails. But the harassment has to be *racial* harassment for you to be able to take legal action. The fact that you're black and your boss is white does not count. The law doesn't allow recovery for that connection; otherwise, every black person would be receiving reparations one lawsuit at a time.

Franklin had been written up for spending too much time on the Internet. Franklin worked in an office job that involved a lot of computer work, and he would frequently jump online to look at the news and sports scores, make travel plans, and otherwise cruise the information highway when he had a few spare minutes—and sometimes when he didn't. Franklin's computer screen faced a part of the work area where his boss could easily see color pictures on his screen. Too bad his job didn't involve color pictures. Franklin felt that he was unfairly harassed because his boss wrote him up for what other people also did. Franklin's boss may very well have been picking on him, but as I explained when he called my office, your boss has the right to make you the example if you're doing something wrong, and most employers find goofing off on the Internet during work hours a problem. This was the only incident Franklin could point to as harassment. Franklin also admitted that the written reprimand probably was not a big deal, considering that he was otherwise an excellent employee and couldn't deny the accuracy of the reprimand. Franklin was just mad that nobody else got in trouble for doing the same thing.

What the law says is that your work environment must be free of racial harassment, and that applies to your coworkers as well as your supervisors if the law feels that your employer could have stopped unlawful harassment and didn't. Examples of this include racial slurs, racial jokes, or any conduct or speech that is "severe and pervasive" and based on your race. (As with just about every aspect of legal discrimination I discuss in this book, while I'm limiting the examples to race because of the focus of the book, the examples also apply to the other protected classes mentioned earlier, as well as conditions covered by your particular state's laws. These may include discrimination or harassment based on sexual orientation, political affiliations, citizenship status, marital status, or personal appearance.)

In the chapter opening, Malik may very well have had a lawsuit. I observed this incident while taking my grandmother out-of-town, and it was one of those rare instances I got to see a potential discrimination lawsuit unfold before my own eyes. Usually, I see the disputed facts on paper long after everything has happened. As a black woman, I was appalled to see these white girls calling this brother "monkey" to his face and laughing. I could see the simmering anger in his demeanor as he quietly made sandwiches, and I could feel his pain of knowing that, while he wanted to slap these white girls silly, in this little town his black behind would not only be out of a job but would be put into the local jail as well.

While my black woman's emotions were processing all this, my dispassionate lawyer's brain wondered about many of the questions I posed at the beginning of the chapter. Unfortunately, declaring a hostile work environment isn't a simple matter. As offensive and upsetting as the behavior of those girls was, if this was the only time something like this ever happened, Malik wouldn't have much of a case if he decided to sue. Worse, what would he really get even if he went to all that trouble? Would it be worth it to burn his bridges in a small town against an influential employer for no more than probably a few thousand dollars? Only Malik would know.

Let's say Malik didn't want to go as far as filing a lawsuit, but he wanted to demand that the behavior stop. Would writing a letter to his supervisor or human resources be a good idea? It depends. It's one of those judgment calls where you have to consider what that will get you where you work. A young friend of mine, a black woman, was being sexually harassed by her boss. On advice from some of her family members she wrote a letter to her boss outlining the behavior and demanding that it stop. The next day her boss fired her. Yes, that was totally and completely illegal—not just the sexually harassing behavior, but also the firing that would be considered illegal retaliation. But my friend was far too concerned with finding another job to go that route. It wasn't that she was wrong to write a letter, but demand letters—where you outline a behavior and demand that it stop—in the hands of someone other than an attorney can be very dangerous.

The advantages to suing are obvious—the chance for closure, justice, punishment, redemption, purging, and, of course, the almighty dollar bill. The news is filled with stories of huge verdicts and companies brought to their knees, but you don't see the negatives in the movies.

In the year 2000, plaintiffs filed more than 259,000 civil complaints in the United States district courts. A *civil complaint* is one where a private individual or group sues another private party, as opposed to a criminal matter where the government brings a matter against an individual. According to the United States Department of Justice, about 41,000 of those complaints involved a civil-rights-related issue such as discrimination in employment, housing, welfare benefits, or voting rights. Of all these civil rights complaints, only 1,652 of them went to trial, with 80 percent of those heard by a jury. The average amount of time elapsed from filing the claim to deposition to trial was 14 months, which of course does not include any appeal that may have taken place. U.S. Department of Justice statistics show that plaintiffs (the people bringing the lawsuit in the first place) won only 34 percent of the verdicts in 2000. Of the 545 plaintiffs who won their trials, 76 percent of them were awarded monetary damages, with half of these awards being $155,500 or less.

What these statistics show is that for employees who feel discriminated against and who take their claims all the way through a federal trial (where discrimination lawsuits under Title VII are typically tried) only about one in three are able to convince a judge or jury they were discriminated against. Of those who won in court, the average amount of money was not enough to live on for any meaningful period of time, especially when you consider that your attorney will take one third to one half of what you recover. Settlements are much harder statistics to track because they are usually signed under a confidentiality agreement, but my educated guess, based on the settlement amounts I've seen, is that the average settlement is considerably lower than the average amount plaintiffs win in a trial verdict.

As someone mostly on the defense end of lawsuits (which means representing the employers who are sued by their employees), I think a person looking for money and vindication from her employers has only slightly better odds of winning than when she buys five dozen Powerball tickets.

Steps in a Lawsuit

Here's a bare bones overview of what happens when someone decides to file a lawsuit. Every lawsuit is different depending on the claims filed, the facts, the lawyer you hire, and more. But all lawsuits, regardless of claims, go a similar route. First, you shop around for an attorney to take your case. If your case looks good and you're willing to take the time to put in the legwork, you find an attorney to take your case. Either before you find an attorney or shortly after doing so, you file a complaint with the EEOC to preserve your right to bring a lawsuit under Title VII. It's possible to file a discrimination suit without doing so, but it makes a tough burden of proof even tougher if you have to assert a discrimination claim without asserting a Title VII claim. Once you find an attorney to take your case, he spends a lot of time going over the facts with you so that he can file a complaint to start the lawsuit in federal court, which is where most discrimination lawsuits are heard because Title VII is federal law. After your employer files an "answer" to your complaint, then the real paper war (called "discovery") begins. That means that you have to turn over all your documents relating to your claim to the other side and the other side has to do the same for you. Neither side gets to pick and choose what they show—it all comes out in the wash—or else the law prohibits you from using that information if your case goes to trial. It's only in a Perry Mason episode where a party gets to come forward with a surprise document the week of trial.

Every evaluation, every memorandum, every e-mail, every company policy, every magazine article you accidentally leave in your desk drawer, every diary entry relating to work is up for grabs. The expense of copying and producing all these documents comes out of your pocket if you settle, if you win, or if your attorney requires it from your contingency agreement (the contract you enter into with your attorney that says her pay is contingent on you acquiring a settlement or verdict). In addition to preparing all that paperwork, you have to answer questions under court orders called *interrogatories* and show up in some lawyer's office to answer questions from your employer's or former employer's lawyers in what is called a *deposition*. In addition to you answering questions all day long under oath, every person you list as a potential witness can also be deposed by the other side's lawyer whether you like it or not or whether he or she likes it or not.

Since in discovery depositions lawyers can ask questions about anything relevant or likely to lead to admissible and relevant information, you will undoubtedly be asked questions about things that you think are none of anyone's business. (A discovery deposition is what happens when the attorney on the other side of the case questions you under oath without a judge present for the purpose of discovering information potentially relevant to the case.) You may not think it is relevant to your lawsuit that you witnessed your scout leader molesting your best friend when you were eight years old, but if you went to therapy over it, the lawyers will question you to prove the point that your emotional distress was caused by your early childhood trauma and not by your boss promoting every white person in the department over you.

In discovery you'll also find out what your coworkers are willing to say under oath (especially if they still work for the company) versus what they're willing to say to you in the break room when the bosses aren't around, and in depositions you'll get to hear what your boss will publicly say about you to justify whatever adverse employment decision he made that has him being deposed in the first place. In other words, you'll learn just how he plans to run you into the ground before a jury.

After discovery closes comes the part that most plaintiffs' attorneys don't really bother explaining well to their clients. It's the part where the employer's attorneys write a long, detailed document (that they bill thousands of dollars for) called a "motion for summary judgment" that essentially asks the judge to rule on all the claims without wasting time or money taking the claims to trial before a jury or the judge. If the judge denies the motion for summary judgment, you get to take your case to trial. If the judge only issues a partial summary judgment, that means you only go to trial on whatever part of the case the judge leaves in because there are "disputed facts." For example, if you bring claims of discrimination, hostile work environment, and retaliation, the judge can rule that there is no basis for trial on the discrimination and harassment claims, and leave it up to a jury to decide the claim of retaliation. This means that evidence on everything other than the retaliation charge has to stay out of trial.

The worst phone call a plaintiff's attorney has to make to her client is to break the news that the judge granted the defendant's complete motion for summary judgment. That's an especially hard phone call to make if there was a settlement offer on the table that the plaintiff didn't accept. What the judge's order means is that unless you appeal (an expensive and time-consuming endeavor that your original attorney may not agree to take on), you've lost before the trial begins. It's the equivalent of the NBA commissioner saying before the start of the NBA finals, "Sorry, but we don't even need to have a championship tournament because Team X is so vastly superior to Team Y that it would be a waste of time and money, because even on the off chance Team Y wins we would still give the championship trophy to Team X." Because summary judgment happens only after depositions and written discovery have taken place, a plaintiff who loses on summary judgment feels a lot like Team X, suited up for a chance to win the big game and not even being allowed to play.

If, as a plaintiff, you survive summary judgment, then you get the opportunity to go to trial. You get the joy of sitting through the grueling weeks of preparing for and enduring one of the most stressful times of your life, while a jury not of your peers (because you will almost always have a mostly white jury in a federal trial) holds the final answer to whether you win and if so, how much.

My years of representing employers has showed me how much more the deck is stacked against the plaintiff from Day One if the employer is a big company. Big companies may not like big legal bills, but they will pay them month after month to keep from paying an undeserving plaintiff one dime. With rare exceptions, an employer who is being sued by an employee, or former employee, never thinks the person deserves anything. When they do decide to settle it's almost always defense counsel who has to walk them down that road, because employers practically never believe they discriminate and don't want to do anything that concedes that they do—which in their minds a settlement does.

A lot of people think it is unfair that lawyers get to walk away with so much of your money. But hey, let's be clear: if not for your lawyer, you wouldn't have the $16,000 in the first place. After all, if talking to your employers by yourself was working, then you wouldn't have gotten demoted, fired, spit on, or whatever it is that drove you to a lawyer's office in the first place, now, would you?

Your Personality Type and Whether to Sue

When it comes down to deciding whether to file a lawsuit, your motivation really does matter. If you're a survivor, there is no good reason to file a lawsuit against your employer or former employer. It's just going to direct a giant spotlight right in your direction, and you're not the kind of brother or sister who can handle it. You're just not built that way. You want to come and go to work, and the only disruption you want in your work world is if you decide to change jobs. Even that is something a survivor typically wants to do with as little fanfare as possible.

If you're a striver, you better do a fabulous cost-benefit analysis of exactly what it will net you in the short run and what it will net you in the long run because, as I frequently tell witnesses during preparation for their first depositions, litigation is war and your guns may not be as big as you think they are. A thriver may win his skirmish and end up losing the war. If you're trying to get ahead in your particular workplace, or even in the profession or industry you work in, no matter how many laws against retaliation exist, no one's career is going to benefit from filing a lawsuit against his employer.

It won't matter how right you are, and except for rare instances, it won't even matter how egregious your boss's behavior was. You will have broken the code. We in the black community know all about that. As soon as a prominent black man goes down in flames for either failing to keeping his hands where they are supposed to be (that is, off a woman who is not his wife or off money that is not his own), then our collective community starts pointing fingers at what black woman or white man brought him down. Nobody likes tattletales, no matter how justified the telling may be.

Thrivers are going to lead with heart first when it comes to going the lawsuit route. They don't embarrass or scare easily, so the pitfalls of taking it to the streets don't paralyze them the way they would for their other black coworkers. It's not that a thriver necessarily operates from a higher sense of integrity than a survivor or a striver; in fact, an individual may operate from less. In the handful of times I've seen a black employee file a discrimination claim that I felt was strictly just for the money, it's usually a person I would classify as a thriver with no fear of the downside and retribution that may come her way. A thriver, whether operating from integrity or not, is just not going to care in the end if she only ends up with a settlement of $3,000 or a jury verdict of $8,000 if she feels she had her day of glory and theater. She got flair and don't care.

Regardless of whether you are a survivor, striver, or thriver, there are certain bottom-line considerations to be taken into account if you are driven to pursue the lawsuit route. A basic one is to make sure that if you do find yourself feeling discriminated against or racially harassed, you find your company's Equal Opportunity policy and follow it to the letter. In other words, if your company's EEOC policy says that you are to report a complaint to your immediate supervisor or human resources manager, then those are your choices. Deciding that you would rather report the complaint to the nice brother or sister supervisor in another department, or to some other employee, may be just the out your employer uses to say that he didn't know there was a problem in the first place. (A recent lawsuit, *Faragher v. City of Boca Raton*, created a defense that allows employers to avoid or reduce liability if they can show that the company had an antidiscrimination policy with an adequate reporting mechanism and the employee failed to use it. Although companies and defense attorneys can use the *Faragher* defense as bludgeon to beat back a claim, I'm a fan of the defense when it is correctly used because it is only fair.)

If you really think that where you worked is whacked, then you should give them a chance to fix it before you run off and file a lawsuit. Yes, you take the chance that you get blown off or treated worse, but you also take the chance that it gets better, not just for yourself but for the other people in a similar situation. This remedy can be a whole lot faster and potentially a lot less painful.

Reporting your problems also puts your company on notice that, if it is being discriminatory in some way or allowing a discriminatory environment to breed, it better fix it because the next time it has to deal with it may be on the responding end of a lawsuit.

I don't believe in idle threats involving the law—more often than not, I think there are better ways to handle situations first. But if you genuinely think that the lawsuit route is going to be a recourse you take down the line, the first place you start is with complaining according to your company's policies.

Can You Hear What I Hear?

My observation is that when people have been discriminated against, the thing they really need is to feel heard. They want to feel as if they had a fighting chance to tell their side or make their case or just vent about what they perceive as unjust action. Employers could cut some complaints or lawsuits off at the knees if they would just have a conversation with a black employee as soon as they get the information that the employee is having problems regarding race in the workplace. Here, as in other areas of life, so much could be resolved quickly through good communication. When the communication turns out to be not so good, sometimes the song just needs to be sung, even if it's a little bit off-key.

10

BRIDGE OVER TROUBLED WATERS

■

Patrick worked in a restaurant as an assistant chef. He worked more hours than part-time, but not enough hours to be officially full-time. Patrick figured he worked long enough and hard enough to be considered full-time, despite the fact that he didn't get benefits. Patrick figured that restaurants were informal places where things were worked out, unlike some fancy-pants office job where people had a lot of stupid rules and regulations to follow. When Patrick, the only black on the kitchen staff, refused to chop some zucchini because he didn't think it fit in the featured entrée, the head chef tried to send Patrick home for the night. Patrick argued back and got fired on the spot. Worse yet, when he tried to get unemployment benefits, he found out that he was ineligible because he wasn't a full-time employee at the restaurant.

Head First or Feet First

Sometimes, the best thing that can happen to you is to get fired. Believe it or not, what can seem like the single most humiliating, painful, scary event in your life can be the most liberating. You don't want to make it a habit, and it's certainly not something you brag about on your resume, but it sometimes happens. When it does, you pick yourself up and you move on.

I got fired from my first job out of college. Carried my happy black behind halfway across the country to work for a big city newspaper and left four months later, hating the city, the city editor, and the newspaper. I know that the experience was the first step toward telling me that, while I loved to write and loved to meet and talk to people, I wasn't cut out for the structure of the daily newspaper business. Because I was so young and it was my first job out of college, I didn't spend any time considering whether being a reporter brought me joy or if I was great at it. I just got another job doing the same thing elsewhere. Sometimes a firing is a gift that can be a blessing in disguise, but only if you pause long enough to look at what the blessing really is.

As I write this, an acquaintance of mine works for a company that has laid off the equivalent of a small town in the past year. He is probably one of the only ones who is mad that he has avoided four different rounds of layoffs. Why doesn't he just quit? Because his company is offering generous severances packages, enough to finance his beloved dream business, and he would rather have that than quit and get nothing but a last paycheck. He's a thriver disguised as a survivor, so when his layoff comes— and it surely will—he'll see it for the blessing it is.

There are only two ways to leave a job—you quit or you get fired. Sure, technically, you could be laid off or your company could go under or you could retire, but any way you slice it, if you're an at-will employee you either do the Electric Slide out on your own, or you start hearing the slow jams come on at the end of the party when you know your host wants you gone.

I've always envied people who have employment contracts. They have defined, clearly identified periods of working relationships—usually a year, when the rubber meets the road unless one of the parties wants to reenlist, so to speak.

Most working Americans will, as at-will employees, have a more haphazard relationship with our employers. From day to day, week to week, month to month, year to year, you wonder if the blade hovers over your neck. Or you don't worry and then, seemingly out of the blue, the guillotine slices your head off anyway.

I'm always amazed, however, at the black people I know who operate without a healthy strain of paranoia in the workplace. Recently a friend of mine, in a fit of rage, threw a coffeepot at a coworker. Hot coffee and flying glass went everywhere. A mediation was scheduled. In between picking up shards of glass and waiting for the mediation, brother man never wavered in his belief that everything would be fine and they wouldn't fire him. He threw the coffeepot at a white coworker for using the word *nigger* in front of him, and his only concern was that his boss would try to force him to shake the white guy's hand. The combination of losing a job at the age of 21 and seeing employment litigation lawsuits everyday made me in awe of my friend's calm. He was right. He didn't get fired, but I still think he needs to look over his shoulder.

This chapter is for figuring out how to survey the lay of the land when you're either ready to bounce, you just got canned, or you expect that it is coming around the corner.

Skin Is In, But What Color?

The funny thing about race in America is that most whites think our black skins protect us from getting the pink slip, with the general assumption being that employers don't want to court a lawsuit. (Pardon the pun.) In comparison, many blacks feel that our skin color makes us stand out when the workplace executioner comes looking for bodies.

Assumptions don't matter. Reasons matter even less when your employer decides to put your head on the chopping block. Any way it happens, it feels like a dull knife.

On the other hand, deciding to leave under your own steam is a tough decision too, if you're leaving because something smells rotten in the apple barrel. Most people who leave for new jobs with more money, more prestige, more everything, and absolutely love their work probably aren't reading this far into this book.

In the workplace, as a black person, you have a lot of considerations when it comes to job security. I've mentioned people who are survivors throughout this book as if there is only one kind. Some people are survivors because their natural attitude is one of temperance. They're the people who usually drive the speed limit, pay their bills on time, and do all the right things at the right times for the right reasons. When that type of black survivor gets the boot, it's usually a performance issue, pure and simple. If you're the kind of black survivor who is working in a fundamentally fair place, you won't get fired until your performance becomes problematic enough to register on your bosses' radar screen. (There are times when straight-up racists target survivors anyway, but fortunately for these types, strivers and thrivers make more attractive targets because they are "uppity" blacks.) For someone who typically operates as a survivor, getting the ax for a performance issue can seem like the end of the world because it symbolizes the ultimate mark of personal failure.

For blacks who typically operate as strivers and always look for the next opportunity to advance, being fired can seem like someone is hauling them right off the ladder of success. Even though thrivers tend to be the most standout kind of black in the workplace, I've always found that strivers are the undercover militants, especially when they get fired. You see, strivers—unlike thrivers—are the ones who bought into the concept that hard work is enough and the blacks who complain about racism are just making excuses. Strivers think that right up until they get the ax or the demotion, and then they practically want to march on Washington.

Back in the day of the forefront of the civil rights movement (and before), black Americans wrestled with the issue of *assimilation* versus desegregation. In simplistic terms, someone who wants to assimilate wants to morph her differences into the collective mainstream. "I'm not a black architect, I'm an architect who happens to be black." Someone who is a fan of desegregation isn't trying to blend in, she's just trying not to be excluded. "I don't care whether you view me as a black architect or an architect who is black, I just want to make sure my black behind has a fair opportunity to be admitted to architecture school." When a striver realizes that the playing field isn't fair and assimilation isn't taking, it can get ugly. In other words, when a striver has to ask Langston Hughes's age-old question, "What happens to a dream deferred?" she begins to feel betrayed and bitter and to wonder if the societal promises of fairness and equality are nothing more than a raisin in the sun.

A black thriver (who usually is about two beats off the company tune anyway) may not be as surprised by a termination when it comes, but he's usually more upset that the white man has the power to put him in the ultimate one-down position. A black thriver, depending on his personality and temperament, will more visibly and directly proclaim just what he feels about his job, his supervisor, and the screwing over he feels he's getting. It's not that thrivers are immune from being surprised by a termination. A thriver can get totally sideswiped too. It's just that his reaction of surprise usually won't be a product of naïveté or trust. Thrivers have great clarity about the politics of the workplace and their place in that dynamic, both individually and as black employees.

Red Flags to Cover Your Butt

What are the red flags that warn you that termination may be coming down the pike? Operating as a driver means paying attention to these warning signs. They may seem obvious, but I am always amazed at the people who say they never saw the firing coming and then, after asking them a few questions, you realize they were just straight-up living at the intersection of Denial Road and Oblivious Boulevard.

Red Flag #1: Criticisms from your boss suddenly start showing up in writing, when criticisms were previously verbal or informal.

Actually, any switch in communication style from your boss should alert you that something is up. If your supervisor, for example, is the type who stops by your work station to talk about your work and then he suddenly starts using e-mail as his primary means of communication, look at the circumstances to see if you should be worried. Like most things in life, it's all about context. For example, if your boss changed to an office farther away or acquired new duties or is going through a divorce, the switch to e-mail may just be circumstantial. But if you see her still communicating freely with Jake, your white cubicle neighbor, chances are there is something up with you.

Basically, if your boss starts communicating with you in writing, or if you start a new job and find yourself receiving written criticisms left and right, you need to consider the possibility that it may be a warning sign of bigger trouble down the road.

One of the key things employment defense attorneys rely on in building a defense is the personnel file of a person bringing a discrimination lawsuit. Unfortunately, the more your personnel file is filled with write-ups and reprimands and written warnings, the easier it will be for the employer to show a legitimate nondiscriminatory reason (one of the legal standards) for doing whatever it is you are suing over in the first place.

Therefore, don't take changes in communication and increased negative feedback lightly. They mean something. They may mean that your boss is overworked or is pissed at you because you spilled Grape Nehi on his rug at the company party at his house, or it may be that you work for someone who likes to exert his "Boss Authority" on paper every chance he gets.

Ask questions about the change in communication style, or ask the person communicating differently some questions. If the answers leave you with a funny feeling, let your fingers get smudged with newsprint shopping for another job (or at least another job in the company) once you determine that it's a you thang rather than a general dissatisfaction that has nothing to do with you.

Red Flag #2: Your key alliances start to undergo changes or your supervisor changes.

Another red flag that is a lot less obvious than the good ol' paper trail is when key alliances start to undergo changes or your supervision changes. What most people don't like to hear, or admit to, is that it does not matter if the supervisor you've had for 12 years loves your work. If the next supervisor doesn't, that can be enough to create some rough waters for you.

No matter what color you are, the bottom line in the workplace is, you are only as good as the last person who evaluates your performance says you are. I've seen situations where really harsh supervisors took over a department and fired a black employee, who then filed a race discrimination claim. As evidence, the fired employees attempted to use the fact that they had glowing evaluations, or at least average ones, until they got this racist supervisor. What usually happens is the company defends itself by saying the new supervisor was a stricter evaluator. In other words, the defense becomes that your glowing reviews all the years before weren't so glowing, you just had an easier boss, which means it's not discrimination when your new boss hates you.

Unfortunately for you, a paper trail can be built as tall as the pyramids behind your back. Your boss doesn't necessarily have to tell you about it or show you the blizzard of nasty comments going on behind closed doors. I know of one brother, a computer specialist, who found out by chance that his boss was planning to pull the plug on his job. He came across at least half a dozen documents outlining not only the how, when, and where, but the details of why—including allegations that he knew nothing about. His job search instantly jumped up to Number One on his "to do" list.

Obviously, this can also work in reverse, too. You get so-so performance reviews for years and then you're lucky enough to get a new boss who just loves your work and gives you great reviews. If you're a driver, you capitalize on that. You use the timing of the better, smarter supervision (because if you look better on paper, the evaluation process had to improve, right?) to figure out what more you want from that job. A supervisor or boss who loves your work and finds your personality a pleasure is a thing of beauty.

When things don't look so good, the point is not to turn into a paranoid wreck who is looking around every corner anticipating a problem or a firing. It's also not about itching for a lawsuit or finding the best way to get back at your boss if you do get fired. In general, it's about heeding the warning signs when you see them, and having a general idea of what your rights and responsibilities are if you do.

Some people have learned just enough about retaliation laws to cloak themselves in protection by filing a complaint with the company or the EEOC when they get a whiff of trouble brewing. Sometimes filing a complaint can slow down the clock and buy you some time to either find another job or work out whatever problem has come up. Other times, your goose is already deep fried, so filing a complaint just gives you another claim to tack on to a lawsuit.

Red Flag #3: Your job or duties change.

When your individual job starts undergoing changes that are not company or department-wide, that might mean you are showing up on someone's radar. I think that is particularly true if your area and level of responsibility shift down instead of up. The change could signal that your boss is trying to say that you're not doing your job well, or that someone else can do it better. When your work responsibilities shift up, that's when you need to look at your circumstances individually. In most cases, it's a sign that your boss trusts you and that's a great thing. In some cases, it's a sign that you're being set up to be broken down. Again, there is no blanket way to know if that's the case other than listening, watching, and observing how others are handled. If your job is changed altogether to a lateral (or lesser) position, then you really need to take that as a red flag that something hinky may be going on. It's one of the things that can be an 85 percent issue or a 15 percent issue. In other words, you've got to investigate the underlying reason for why this is happening and what the future implications of it are.

What You Can Expect When You Leave

If you're not fired and you choose to leave, what do you have the right to ask from your employer? Every state is different, but employees are entitled to what they accumulated up to the point they quit. By that, I mean that your boss can't get mad at you if you quit and, as a form of retaliation, not pay you for the work you did last week. Your boss can decide, however, that the day you turn in your resignation is the last day she wants you working, and she has no obligation to allow you to work past that day.

Tanya worked at a fast food restaurant as a cashier. She told her manager she was quitting to go work for another fast food place that paid a higher hourly wage. Her manager told

Tanya that, despite her two weeks' notice, he didn't want her to come back once her shift was over. When Tanya came back to the restaurant a few days later to collect her last paycheck, her manager had failed to include payment for the last week she worked. Tanya called a lawyer, saying she wanted her pay for that last week plus the two weeks she was willing to work. Her lawyer informed her that under state wage and hour laws she was entitled to the last week of pay because she actually worked to earn it, but that the law doesn't require you to be paid for time you didn't work. Since Tanya was an at-will employee, her boss had the right to cut off her continued ability to work for that employer.

Unless you are under a contract that requires it, the whole concept of two weeks' notice is a courtesy, not a legal requirement. That's why, even when I have a good relationship with an employer, I quit before I quit. By that I mean I erase all personal e-mails from the system, get rid of private items from my hard drive, and make sure that any personal documents I've casually thrown in my desk drawer are taken home without drawing attention to the fact. The other day, some friends of mine, black and white, and all employment defense attorneys, were joking about how you could guess when we were about to quit. I said if you saw the picture of my grandmother, mother, and dog gone, I was out. One guy said his diplomas off the wall would be our first clue. The other guy said check to see if the photos of his wife and daughters were missing. Another friend jokingly said her office will be gutted.

Take a tip from the employment lawyers. If we clean house first, that might be a good idea for you, too. Because of the type of law we practice, we're aware that you never know how your boss is going to take a resignation, and that the day you give your two weeks' notice could be your last day, period. In fact, if things are shaky at work, it's best to start making the slow, unobtrusive movement of stuff from your workplace to your home. You may get zero advance notice from your boss if she decides to ask you to leave, and sometimes she may barely allow you to get your personal belongings, under her watchful eye, before she escorts you from the building.

I remember how one day, when I was a newspaper reporter, a black female editor was called to the managing editor's office. When she got to his office, she was surprised to find herself fired. What was more surprising to her was that she wasn't even allowed to go back to her desk to clean out her personal items— she was escorted out of the building and a white female editor was sent to retrieve her purse and give it to the fired editor at her car. I wasn't close to the editor and I don't know if she saw the firing coming, but if she didn't, she lost all ability to shield her personal items and papers from prying eyes when her box of private things was sent to her. She also lost access to any pertinent information she might have wanted to print out, should she have wanted to file a discrimination claim.

Cash Out Benefits or Forfeit Them

In addition to any pay you've earned, you need to look at your company policy to see if you have any unused vacation time or if you get paid sick leave. Remember, none of it is a given. It's all dictated by a combination of state law and company policy.

That's pretty much all your company is obligated to give you once you tell them you're hitting the road.

In Missouri, my home state, we have a statute that requires an employer to furnish a "service letter" when you leave employment, regardless of how you leave. Generally, the letter serves as a statement from your employer saying that you worked there, giving your job description and your dates of employment. That could come in handy for an employee who gets fired or quits and needs to verify employment, but doesn't want to list anyone from the company as a reference. (Of course, in volunteering a letter like that to a prospective employer, you may be sending them a red flag that you can't get a good reference from your former employer. Depending on your individual circumstances, you may decide to take that chance.)

Unemployment Benefits Don't Benefit All

Unemployment benefits are governed by statutory law. According to the Department of Labor, less than 40 percent of jobless Americans were able to receive unemployment benefits in the year 2000. For one thing, in just about every state, quitting your job does not entitle you to unemployment benefits. Also, if you receive a severance package from your employer (usually just the equivalent of your pay for a set period of time, such as one week for every year you worked, or a flat two-month severance), it can affect the size of your unemployment benefits and the length of time you receive them. Severance payments are typically deducted from unemployment benefits. Many states also look at the reason why you were terminated to decide if you are eligible. For example, if you were terminated for a reason that would basically be considered a crime, also known as "felonious conduct," you might not be eligible. (Note: Because this is almost entirely governed by state law, it is nearly impossible to know just from reading this chapter whether you would be eligible for unemployment benefits in your state.)

Is a Severance Package in Your Future?

Let's say you get offered a severance package, or you've been terminated and want to know if you're eligible for a severance package.

It should go without saying that if you are fired for doing something that would land you in the penitentiary, then you're probably not going to be in the position to ask your employer for another dime, other than what they already owe you. I know of a case where an employer caught an employee putting some of the employer's product into the employee's car on company time. Unfortunately for the employee, it wasn't the employee's job to load product, and it certainly wasn't in his job description to load it into his own car and drive it home. One pesky, well-placed video surveillance camera caught the employee's beautiful profile, and his job became nothing more than a line on another job application. Did the employer offer the employee a severance package? Indirectly. The employer didn't offer the employee money, but he graciously didn't call the police and have the man arrested. I'd call that a good severance package.

On the other hand, if you're getting terminated for poor performance and you truly believe that it doesn't pass the smell test, ask for severance. For example, if you're the only black person in the department and the boss seems to be overlooking the performance deficiencies of your white coworkers, your employer might be willing to talk severance to keep you from filing a complaint or lawsuit down the line. Of course, the size of the sever-ance will almost never be enough for you to retire on. It might be two weeks' pay or it might be eight months', depending on how vulnerable the employer feels, and you'll almost always be asked to sign a release that waives all future claims and lawsuits.

Is it worth hiring a lawyer to try to get a better severance? In most cases it is not, unless you are in a situation where you believe the intercession of an attorney would get you several more months' severance than doing it on your own. Truthfully, most of the time I think it wouldn't be worth the expense, since whatever you get is split with the attorney. When I was a plaintiff's attor-ney, I had a client for whom I was able to negotiate an eight-month severance package because the employer did such a bad job of firing the man, it started to look like something other than performance might have been the real issue. Without him hiring me, he might have only gotten two months. But in hiring me, by the time I took out my cut and expenses, he really only received about four months of severance. For him, it was worth it, not just from a financial standpoint, but to make it a point of pride with his former company that he wasn't going to give them a free pass for unfair treatment.

The lesson I learned from that experience is that people don't have a very realistic idea of what it means when they do hire a lawyer. Hiring a lawyer totally changes the dynamic. Sometimes it makes it a lot worse because your employer or former employer is so pissed you took it outside that he becomes totally inflexible. Or sometimes he becomes so intimidated or irritated that he'll throw a little more money at the situation to either make it go away quickly or keep it from escalating into a much more pub-lic, much more expensive showdown. In any case, merits don't have a whole lot to do with the final outcome.

Unless you're leaving your job for more cash or more cachet, it's never easy to leave. If you get fired, it never feels good, regardless of how necessary the break was in the big picture of your life. If you leave because you're unhappy, especially because you feel you didn't get a break because of your race, that feeling can seep into your soul and leave you unsettled for years to come.

As I said at the beginning of the book, how you start is how you finish—and I believe that how you finish can affect your next start. If you can, make choices that leave you with dignity and that allow you to walk out on your own terms. Even if that doesn't happen and you find yourself walking out on your employer's terms, you always have the right and the duty to yourself to walk out with your head held high.

11

FEELING DOWN BUT NOT OUT

■

Next to the CEO and the vice president of the company, Edward is the highest-paid person in his Fortune 500 company. There are only a small handful of black executives in the country that have Edward's kind of juice or make his kind of bank outside of the entertainment and sports industries.

Although Edward sometimes works 16-hour days and frequently has to travel for his job, the one thing that he always does is take his five-mile-a-day run. Period. Without fail. Whether he's at home or Hong Kong or Paris or Toronto, he exercises his body, knowing that his mind and spirit are stronger because of it.

How you start is how you finish. It applies to so many things—relationships, jobs, new situations. As I've gotten older, I've realized that the saying is more about the spiritual than the physical start to a new beginning.

If I go into a work situation believing I'm doing the exact job I'm perfect for, then chances are when I leave the job or get promoted or transferred, it will be a better ending or transition than if I started off that same job feeling like I was lucky to even get the interview in the first place.

Ultimately, your job isn't just one part of your life, it is a reflection of every choice you've ever made. I make this bold statement because I believe everything is connected to everything else. It's no coincidence that ambitious, hard-working people, regardless of race, make more money than people who desire nothing more than doing the least amount of work for the most amount of money. Sure, there are lazy CEOs who are born into wealth and hard-working janitors who develop calluses from what they do. My point isn't about deserving what you get, it's about getting what choices create, even the choices that seem unrelated to that job.

Edward runs his five miles every day because, ultimately, he is an instinctive striver who aims to be a driver. He knows that to keep his mind sharp and his goals sharper, he has to have an outlet for stress. He also knows that as superficial as it may be, a fit, healthy black man will command more respect from everyone he deals with than one who looks like he can be toppled by one more helping of fast food or one more cigarette.

I began this book by saying that a black person in America needs to start thinking about what makes her or him happy before she or he enters the job market. While you can change your mind midway, there is just no reason to be on a path you hate if you give thought to who you are and what you want from life.

Last year I started doing yoga. At the start of every class, Kathleen, my yoga instructor, starts off saying, "Set your intention. Say your prayer for whatever you need from class today." When Kathleen asks that, I have to consciously think about what I need for that class. Stamina? Energy? Flexibility? Just to get through class, even though I might feel like a soft bed or a cool drink would be better?

In a nutshell, setting your intention is what you have to do as a black person who wants to succeed in the working world. You don't just set your intention once. You set it every day, every year, and at every stage of your career. As you grow and change, your intentions grow and change. Whether you are a survivor, a striver, or a thriver, intention is the one thing always within your power, regardless of the dynamics that you do not control. Intention is what turns a survivor, striver, or thriver into a driver, and intention is one part of your work life you do have the power to control and nurture.

Throughout this book I've addressed the 15 percent difference that defines being a black person in the workplace; however, I never lose sight of the fact that we are all 100 percent human. No matter how many ways you define yourself, keeping mental, physical, emotional, and spiritual balance should be your top priority for maintaining a healthy work life.

At the end of the day no one can tell you exactly how to deal with your boss, your company, or your employer. So much of what it means to be black in America, especially a working black, is to accept and not feel crushed by the fact that the dynamics are so much larger than you are. Maintaining a healthy balance in your life will help carry you through the hard times and succeed during the good ones.

Yesterday, I heard a white secretary complaining; she was upset about a computer freezing up. The same day I got a call from a friend who is a black attorney; she wanted me to help calculate the likelihood of her being fired by the end of the year. Stress may be stress, but from where I sit, it seems that whites at work usually get stressed over tangible irritations. While all employees get stressed out over concrete annoyances such as computers freezing, black employees often pile on top of that stress the added stress that the subtle but powerful nuances being a minority in the workplace generates.

Society will indeed be equal when black people have the same peace of mind that whites do, so we can just let life happen, without the added stress of hidden agendas constantly tugging at the edges of our consciousness. We still live in a society where being black is a consideration that impacts every aspect of our existence.

Walter, a black accountant, was in a low-grade panic because he had been having trouble with Jennifer, his white supervisor. Walter sent Jennifer an e-mail requesting permission for the go-ahead on a time-sensitive project, and she hadn't responded despite the fact that the two of them had passed in the hall several times and chatted in the company cafeteria. Jennifer had even responded promptly to Walter's e-mails regarding other current projects. When Walter finally mustered the nerve to go ask Jennifer directly about the new project, Jennifer said yes without hesitation, stating that she had just forgotten to get back to Walter. Walter read Jennifer's lack of response as confirmation of his lack of job security.

E-mail makes many people expect to hear back from others more quickly, and feel slighted by others who don't respond promptly. But blacks suffer from obsessively thinking we're out of sync with what's going on with our white supervisors.

In some ways, this is the most important chapter of this book because this one's all about you and the things you can control to improve your life, whether you're a survivor, a striver, or a thriver. You can file every complaint, bring every lawsuit, fight every fight, but you can't control the outcome.

As a driver, however, what you can control is your ability to live your life without compromise in an environment you can alter, but not fix. In other words, you can learn to control your response to what you can't control, similar to the serenity prayer used in twelve-step programs where you ask your higher power to grant you the serenity to accept the things that can't be changed, and the courage to change the things that can be changed, and the wisdom to know the difference. That should probably be the workplace mantra for blacks, too.

I've read more than once that when a pilot flies, the pilot spends most of his time correcting the flight plan while navigating between takeoff and landing points. This is because between wind, weather, and dozens of other subtle yet significant factors that can't be predicted, a pilot has to spend much of the flight correcting any deviation that takes the airplane off track.

As a black person in America who works, keeping on top of a healthy, balanced lifestyle is critical for moving forward and keeping that 15 percent difference to a minimum. Trying to maintain that healthy balance becomes a necessary way to constantly set your intention and keep on course.

Internalizing Is a Form of Depression

Depression and job stress can lead to quiet, unconscious ways of taking yourself out of this life early.

I think one of the reasons that black Americans are disproportionately more religious than the rest of America is because the hope of a better afterlife is what many of us have been led to hold onto. Most of us have to believe in this concept of a better world beyond. We had to believe that as slaves, we had to believe that during Jim Crow, and we especially have to believe it now when everything is supposed to be equal but we see every day that it's not. How can we survive today, in this world, in this life, if we look at the routine, unblinking, unthinking, unrepentant discrimination that we deal with daily in every area of our lives, if we don't cling desperately to the idea of hope?

I've attended too many funerals of my people where that was exactly the theme of the eulogy—that the pain and the hopelessness and the life of struggle would reap its reward on the other side. Rap and hip-hop aren't anything more than modern-day Negro spirituals sung by our youth.

A white coworker of mine came rolling into my office recently full of chit-chat about the fact that the D.C. sniper was a black man. "Didn't see that one coming," was the sentiment he expressed and the one expressed all over the country. After all, it's not a "black crime" to shoot randomly or murder serially. Nope, we do garden-variety black-on-black crimes, with a few smash and grabs thrown in to break up the monotony.

I pointed out to my coworker that white America might want to be a little scared that this might start a trend. After all, most of the employees and former employees who shoot up workplaces because they feel they've been treated badly are, statistically speaking, both white and male. Just think what would happen if blacks who felt treated badly in the workplace took up guns instead of EEOC complaints. He left my office muttering, "It would be bad all the way around."

Fortunately for America, but unfortunately for black Americans, we take our stress, anger, and hopelessness and we turn it inward. According to a recent study, blacks have higher death rates than whites for 8 of the 10 leading causes of death—heart disease, cancer, stroke, unintentional injuries, flu and pneumonia, diabetes, HIV/AIDS, and cirrhosis of the liver. David R. Williams, a sociologist at the University of Michigan Institute for Social Research (the world's largest academic survey and research organization), says that the racial gap between the health of whites and blacks is no different now than it was in 1950 and in part links that gap to "the historic legacy of racism."

Not to be flip, but that makes sense to me. If I can't hit my boss for being a racist jerk (or at the very least an insensitive one), my blood pressure is going to consistently go up, which increases my risk for a heart attack or stroke. If I constantly see my white coworkers treated with grace and dignity through every screwup while I know my mistakes put me one step closer to the firing line, chances are that I will tend to smoke or drink more or eat more or act more recklessly when I'm away from work, which increases my risk of cancer, heart disease, accidents, and so forth. You get the point.

Blacks have higher mortality rates than whites until the age of 85, according to the National Center for Health Statistics. The disparities between blacks and whites in morbidity include blacks being three times more likely than whites to have diabetes and having a 40 percent higher rate of heart disease; the infant mortality rate for blacks is twice that of whites regardless of education, marital status, or income. It doesn't take a Ph.D. to know that living a more stressful life without healthy outlets leads to more stress.

That's why as a black community, we tend to get only part of the equation better than the rest—we work on the spiritual aspect but often let the physical, mental, and emotional ways of dealing go unchecked.

Being black is a full-time job. Blacks get hit with it all—a higher incidence of bad health, lower access to good health care, and more stresses to start the vicious cycle all over again. In fact, studies show that blacks of all income levels tend to get less attentive medical care than whites.

So, how does that relate to work? Easy: the one thing that contributes most to an unhealthy lifestyle is stress. You know how it goes. If you're stressed, you look for an outlet to relieve it such as smoking, overeating, taking drugs, gambling, overspending, or getting abusive.

A study that came out of Finland in 2002 said stress can double your risk of dying of heart disease. The study showed that people who reported persistent stress due to work, low job security, or few career opportunities had the same level of risk for fatal heart attacks as people who smoke and don't exercise. Apparently, high job stress was associated with being overweight and having high cholesterol. That might explain why, compared to the over-all population, blacks have more weight problems and higher cholesterol. I don't know about the folks in Finland (I don't even know if they have any blacks in Finland), but I do know that if you're black in America, you got stress all the way around.

So you have greater stress in your life. Now, what can you do to help yourself do battle at work when necessary, and to have the emotional, spiritual, and physical stamina to carry on all day, every day?

Working It Out While Talking It Over

Marissa is a time bomb waiting to go off. She's a 30-some-thing black employee who works for the government and has had half a dozen screaming matches with fellow employees, all black. Her supervisor, a white man, keeps ordering medi-ations and in-house counseling sessions. Marissa is on edge, and everyone who works with her is on edge when they see her temper about to flare. Everyone assumes it will take Marissa going off on a white person for the boss to really do anything about it. She clearly needs to seek out a mental health care professional. It might be some physical or psy-chological problem that causes her to act out, or it may be that Marissa is just a bitch. Either way, she needs to have someone help her get a grip. Without taking a serious dip in the anger management pool, Marissa is in no position to stave off dealing with any work-related difficulties that come her way.

There are certain cultural realities that plague our community and put us at an even greater risk for stress. One is that we tend not to seek out help when we need it, or even to think we need it in the first place. "I ain't crazy." "I'm not talking to some white person about my problems." "It's nobody's business what I'm thinking." "It's not that bad." "Therapy and that kind of foolishness is for white folks." "I'll just pray on it." "I can handle it."

Prayer is great. So are supportive friends and family. Our own internal strength is the best of all, but sometimes we need to seek out another person to talk to—a voice from outside our daily life to give perspective.

If you don't do it because it's good for you or because you might need it, think of it from a legal perspective. Juries award for damages. The bigger the damages, the bigger the monetary award. Damages have to be proved. One of the ways you can prove damages is by showing you were so mentally and emotionally traumatized you had to seek therapy.

Therefore, if you decide to seek out a counselor or therapy, don't look at it as the boss or white folks driving you to therapy. Look at it as the natural aftermath of a stressful injury. If you got hit by a car or came down with a painful physical disease, you wouldn't look at it as moral failing because you had to see a doctor. That's the way to look at excessive stress.

I've always felt that, with the higher level of stress and abuse black Americans go through, therapy should be free for anyone who seeks it out as a tax the rest of society has to pay. But I know that one very true concern about going to seek therapy is that when you're stressed from every direction, the last thing you want to do is bare your soul to a white person. Not only do you want someone who automatically understands what you're talking about, you just don't want to be in the position of being judged by yet another person not of your own background. You're not willing to give someone that kind of power.

There are black mental health care providers. You have to look harder for them, but they exist. (See the Resources section for a helpful Web site.)

Spiritual Journey to Keep You on Your Path

As I said, many blacks count themselves as regular churchgoers. What if you're not? Am I recommending going to church? Nope, not at all. I personally think that everyone needs to find her own basis for spirituality, and do whatever it is that nurtures her soul. If Jesus Christ is your path, then find ways to incorporate more of that path into your daily work life. In other words, don't just go to church on Sunday. Become more active in your church or do more volunteer work. Perform your own set of spiritual rituals that makes you feel like your time on this earth matters and that collecting that paycheck isn't the only use you have. One friend of mine is a church usher and finds that her regular church attendance and other activities help her cope when she goes to work, because she feels she is working as an instrument of Christ.

If you're not a Christian, don't let Christians make you think that it's the only path to salvation if you're black. Explore other options, whether that is Buddhism, Islam, or Yoruba. Don't let the majority (which includes the majority of black people) stop you. If you need to chant or say a mantra before you go to work in the morning, do it. It's nobody else's business who that chant is to or what it includes.

Religion is one of those no-no topics to get into with blacks if you're not exactly on the same page. If you don't believe in

God or a higher power, then look to something that provides spiritual sustenance. If it's not the Bible, or Iyanla Vanzant, then do volunteer work. Seeing a whole bunch of people less fortunate than yourself is a good way to put work stresses in perspective, as well as build some spiritual muscles you might have forgotten you had.

The Body Tells Your Whole Story

Another major area of our lives we have to put more of a priority on is the physical. As black Americans, we can't afford to go to work at anything less than optimal health because, as that Finnish study I referred to earlier concludes, people with more job stresses already have double the risk of heart disease.

At least the federal government is getting hip to the fact that it's ridiculous there is no better overall health care for blacks than there was 50 years ago. The Department of Health drew up a federal mandate in 2000 that says by 2010, health care disparities should be eliminated. Starting in the year 2003, the National Institute of Health will no longer review grant proposals for studies that don't say how they will include minorities in clinical trials.

In terms of being proactive, that means that we black Americans have to do our part to make sure our employers can't hit a moving target—and if we're getting exercise, we're moving. It's harder to take down or run over a healthy man or woman than an unhealthy, sickly one. Getting fit and staying fit allows you to be in top shape to manage your workplace experience. That's why we have to walk, run, bike, hike, or dance to music on the radio. We've got to shake our money-makers if we want to make more money and live long enough to enjoy it.

Smoking cigarettes doesn't help us either. As recently as 1998, the U.S. Department of Health and Human Services said that approximately 29 percent of blacks smoke. That's almost one third of us engaging in a destructive activity that just nets us easier access to strokes, heart attacks, and all the other things that just don't seem to hit whites nearly as early, often, or hard as they hit us.

Obesity is another one of those preventable risk factors that affects us more than any other group because we use food as the great equalizer. We eat more and have worse eating habits. We like our chicken greasy, our potatoes buttery, and our vegetables cheesy. And we better have dessert, starting with sweet potato pie and ending with whatever is our mama's specialty.

One of the tolls obesity takes on our community is the epidemic rate of adult diabetes. According to a report in December 2001 from the National Diabetes Education Program at the National Institutes of Health, of the 15.7 million men and women currently diagnosed with diabetes (a number that increases by roughly 800,000 new cases each year), more than half are women and half of those are black. Those high numbers are attributed to the rise of obesity, lack of exercise, and the fact that people are living longer overall.

The Black Women's Health Project reported that out of every 100 black women, 67 are overweight and 38 of those overweight are considered obese, which means they are 20 percent or more above the ideal body weight.

How does this relate to being black in the workplace? Unfortunately, higher stress without healthy ways to cope leads to unhealthy habits and excessive worrying. Eating is a form of stress relief so it's easy to see how sitting on a couch worrying instead of working through stress physically relates to the fact that the death rates for blacks with diabetes are 2.5 times higher than for their white counterparts.

Another physical manifestation of stress is high blood pressure, with studies showing that black men 20 and older have nearly twice the likelihood of having high blood pressure as white men of the same age. High blood pressure is a major heart attack risk factor. According to studies cited in the book *The Black Man's Guide to Good Health*, racial discrimination can be a cause of stress that can lead to high blood pressure.

Strong Mental Health Makes Us Stronger at Work

In an ideal world, the good life of fatty food, tasty liquor, and minimal exertion—with a few cigarettes and recreational drugs thrown in for good measure—would have no impact on health, stress, or vitality. But that's not the case. If you're battling workplace stress, here are a few tips based on what the statistics say particularly affect black folks:

1. Get regular checkups. You may be more stressed than you realize, and a doctor might be able to help nail down ways it is manifesting itself that you aren't even aware of.

2. Take an honest look at the ways you self-medicate and why you do it. Don't fool yourself if you know you eat, drink, smoke, or engage in any harmful activity to excess as a way of distracting yourself from work-based insecurity or discrimination.

3. Stay active. Running your mouth and jumping to conclusions are forms of daily exercise, but they are not the kinds that help

counteract deep-seated stress. Walk, run, bike, dance, take a class, or pick up a sport. Pound that ball, burn up that pavement, or punish that boxing bag. Let the unchecked adrenaline course through your body.

4. Get more sleep. When you're overly stressed you often have trouble going to sleep, or you don't sleep soundly when you do go to sleep. Sleep deprivation doesn't make the day go any better at work. When someone is working on your last nerve and it's not a well-rested nerve, you might find yourself having inappropriate responses that will just make everything worse. According to sleep researchers, most people need 60 to 90 minutes more sleep than they get.

5. Engage in less "groupthink" and more "what do I think." In general, we black people are very much into the collective. I recently had a conversation with a black newcomer to Kansas City, Missouri, who was asking me why he never saw black people at this location or that location. He mistakenly thought there were a lot fewer blacks in the city because of this. I pointed out all the places that are "in" for blacks to go to and that, unfortunately, the places he liked to go weren't "in" for blacks at that time. Part of our stress comes from our assumption that if a large number of blacks say something, it must be so, from music to restaurants to religion to public opinion on an issue. We all have a responsibility to rely on fact rather than sheer opinion for the sake of our peace of mind.

6. Set goals. Don't just set goals in your head, write them on paper and make them specific. Make some easily attainable and small— for example, update your resume by the end of the month—and then set some that allow you to reach beyond your immediate

grasp, for example, open my own jazz bar by my 45th birthday. Writing down your hopes and dreams and the steps you can take toward those hopes and dreams helps you to feel less at the mercy of your employer. It's part of the spiritual component of knowing that you are part of a bigger plan.

The smartest, most successful black striver can find himself smack in the middle of stress overload. The Bible says, to whom much is given, much is required. Those higher requirements can bring on greater stress. In other words, some blacks have stress overload from dealing with discrimination and problems at work, other blacks have it going on so much and so well that the stress from carrying the heavy load of societal success gets to them.

Studies have shown that the short-term effects of stress on performance include:

- Interference with judgment
- Difficulty making good decisions
- Reduction in work enjoyment
- Seeing difficult situations as a threat rather than as a challenge
- Promotion of negative thinking
- Damage to self-confidence
- Narrow attention
- Disrupted focus and concentration
- Difficulty coping with distractions

All the ways that stress can manifest itself are ways that can impair your work performance, and impaired work performance makes you a more likely target for your boss. All in all it's a vicious cycle for anyone to be caught in and it's particularly deadly for a black person to be caught in. That's why it is so critical to get a handle on stress when it rears its ugly head.

"The Runaway Slave"

When I told a friend of mine, a black woman in her 50s, about the topic of this book, she suggested that I have a chapter about the "runaway slave" for blacks who think about working for themselves or starting their own businesses.

She's got a great point. Leaving the white work world is an option. Unfortunately, it's not one that many of us have a lot of experience with thinking about. When I decided to open my own law firm, I had no role models for how to start a business. I had worked for others since the age of 14, I was the daughter of a life-long federal government employee, and the grandchild of people who had always worked for other people. What I learned from the experience of working for myself is more about mentality and courage than anything else. There are books and Web sites where you can gather advice about the details and the business end, but there is no substitute for being the person who has to make it all happen. When I worked for myself, I didn't have the necessary mentality—I didn't have the courage to exist without the security blanket of a regular paycheck and I didn't have the financial or emotional resources to ever feel at ease with that discomfort. My life had not yet prepared me with the confidence that I could do it on my own, and my faith wasn't strong enough to trust that everything would work out. I gave the solo thing a try for a year while having the crutch of a part-time job with another law firm.

In the end, I don't think it was a mistake for me to open my own office, nor to close it when it didn't feel right for me. Deep down, my real desire was to write, so ultimately, all the different paths I've taken as a journalist and as an attorney ended up being steps on this journey with their own set of joys and regrets.

One of my closest friends grew up in Detroit and is the son of a business owner. He grew up seeing nothing but blacks owning their own businesses and succeeding. It was second nature for him to soar with an entrepreneurial spirit. Just like I had no experience seeing blacks work for themselves and do it successfully, he struggled with the concept that blacks should try to do it any other way.

Another alternative to working in primarily white workplaces or working for yourself is to seek out black-owned companies to work for. If you want to work for a big or medium-sized company, obviously those options are easier to find in larger cities with large black populations, such as Detroit, Atlanta, and Dallas. However, people are people and the 85 percent issues matter just as much in black companies. It's about finding the right job, the right career, and the employer that matches what you need. Yes, you might not have to deal with a boss who doesn't "get" you because you're black, but a different kind of cultural bias can kick in. After all, a black executive who spent his summers on Martha's Vineyard may still have a huge disconnect from a brother or sister who spent their summers on the sidewalk with hip-hop and Kool-Aid.

■

The best option for your peace of mind may be to find another way to make a living, other than be a black employee working for a white company. Because I'm a lawyer, it's no surprise that a good deal of my friends are lawyers too, but as well as my lawyer friends and my old journalism friends, my circle of friends includes folks who work full time as astrologers, feng shui consultants, massage therapists, and yoga instructors. Unlike half my friends who are lawyers and would rather be doing *anything* else, none of my friends with nontraditional jobs would rather be doing anything else. Now that's telling.

The most unhappy people I know are the folks who are frustrated because they would rather be doing something else—folks who want to be musicians, teachers, filmmakers, and writers—but who find it easier to work for companies that provide regular paychecks. One of my favorite books is *The Artist's Way* by Julia Cameron. She writes about how many people are frustrated artists trying to quash their artistic spirit because society tells us that we need to have safe, reliable, grown-up jobs. I think this is particularly true of blacks who grew up with parents who had limited opportunities to have good jobs.

Everyone who has a dream has to decide if it's worth it to pursue the dream or let it ride. If you've got a spouse who depends on your regular income and children who expect to be fed, then being a "runaway slave" may not be a viable option. But part of keeping your life in balance is, hopefully, evolving in a way that allows you to make the difficult choices and find a place for your dreams!

Dozens of people have said to me, when they find out I'm a lawyer, "I've always thought about going to law school." My usual response is, "That's interesting, but have you ever thought about being a lawyer?" People usually get a puzzled look on their faces because most people haven't thought what they might want to do past law school graduation. They get caught up in the romantic vision of doing something other than what they are doing, without giving real thought to what they want to do the day after graduation. It's an example of the importance of moving toward something good instead of just away from something bad.

As black people, unfortunately, we have a greater tendency to limit our range of options because, historically, this country has done such a dandy job of limiting options for us first. There is a tale about an elephant trainer who tied one end of a rope around the leg of a baby elephant and the other end of the rope around the base of a tree. The purpose was to keep the baby elephant from wandering away, and the elephant could only walk as far as the rope tied to the tree allowed. Eventually the elephant trainer took off the rope, and the elephant spent the rest of its life never going farther than the length of that rope.

In so many ways, as blacks, we are like that baby elephant. The length of that rope (sort of like a noose) tells us we can be sports heroes and music stars, along with a few safe careers that already include a significant number of blacks, but we still struggle collectively when venturing beyond the confines of that rope.

One of the reasons why it so important to keep mental, emotional, physical, and spiritual balance in your life as a black employee is so you can know when you are feeling reined in. It's also important so you can know and feel when you are soaring to exactly where you want to be.

CONCLUSION

I LOVE BEING BLACK. I DO. I love my people, our style, our culture, and our flavor in the melting pot.

But being black is a full-time job in America, and it's not a job that pays so we each must work it out along the way on our own time.

As I said in the introduction, this world has changed beyond our wildest expectations. A man today can seriously think about staying home with his children in lieu of pursuing a career, while his wife leaves the house every day to go to work. Although that still isn't common, 50 years ago it was science fiction.

Fifty years ago, a black person would not have thought about sitting at the front of the public bus. Now a black person can drive a luxury car past a white person sitting at the bus stop. Again, maybe not the norm, but no longer extraordinary.

Success is the birthright of a black worker entering the workforce today, but discrimination, bigotry, and insensitivity still have place settings at the table of success. In seeing discrimination where none exists, we become our own worst enemy. In ignoring discrimination where it does exist, we are victimized without ever knowing there's been a crime.

My favorite definition of the word *magic* is what happens when intention meets attention. I believe that black employees can create magic in our working lives by knowing what we intend to achieve and by paying attention to how we're getting there.

Happy survivors may never pick up this book because they don't need to know anything more than what the job requires. A desperate survivor may pick up this book wanting to know how to quickly make his or her working world all right again. Strivers—whether content or afraid—might pick up the book because they want any edge that gets them to what they are trying to achieve. Thrivers—whether cruising or fed up—may look at this book as a way to figure out how not to get trampled in the rat race.

But as any black employee who has gotten far enough in her life and career to have picked up this book in the first place should know, we're all in it together and we all have the potential to be drivers. One black person's success is every black person's success. One black person's discrimination is every black person's sorrow. We're role models for each other—regardless of how much money or prestige our job has compared to someone else's. With our hair, clothes, speech, and attitude, we make the workplace browner, and the workplace is better for it.

Ultimately, you own your own experience as a black employee. You have to think, plan, prepare, observe, investigate, savor, and orchestrate every aspect of your job and career—and then, when necessary, you've got to do it all over again. Whether you're a street sweeper or a CEO, your job should reflect the glory of all the good choices you've made and all the adversities you've weathered along the way. The 15 percent issues will always arise, but you can achieve good results that are 100 percent yours. Remember the rules of the road to arrive at a successful working life:

- How you start is how you finish.
- The proof is in the pudding, not the pudding mix.
- No matter what comes your way, you can create career magic when you combine intention with attention.

Good luck!

RESOURCES

■

Books

For Employment and Job Hunting

Bolles, Richard Nelson. *What Color Is Your Parachute: A Practical Manual for Job-Hunters and Career-Changers*. Berkeley, CA: Ten Speed Press, updated yearly.
■ This widely used guide for job hunters and people changing careers has been updated and republished every year since 1976. It is particularly useful for those already in the workforce.

Covey, Stephen R. *Seven Habits of Highly Effective People*. New York: Simon & Schuster, 1989.

■ This classic book gives tools to improve personal effectiveness and leadership.

Deluca, Matthew J. *Best Answers to the 201 Most Frequently Asked Interview Questions*. New York: McGraw-Hill, 1996.
■ This book gives you an idea of what employers commonly ask and what they are looking for, so that you can prepare for a job interview.

Johnson, Spencer, M.D., and Kenneth H. Blanchard. *Who Moved My Cheese? An Amazing Way to Deal with Change in Your Work and in Your Life*. New York: G. P. Putnam's Sons, 1998.
■ This is a little book about the big idea of figuring out your role in the dynamic of people trying to get ahead.

Sinetar, Marsha. *Do What You Love, the Money Will Follow*. New York: Dell, 1987.
■ This book gives step-by-step advice in finding the best work for you, according to your needs and talents.

Other Helpful Books

Adrienne, Carol. *The Purpose of Your Life: Finding Your Place in the World Using Synchronicity, Intuition, and Uncommon Sense*. New York: Eagle Brook, 1999.
■ This book emphasizes the importance of thinking outside the box to find your life's path.

Cameron, Julia. *The Artist's Way: A Spiritual Path to Higher Creativity*. New York: Putnam, 1992.

- This is a great book on how to free yourself from being a "blocked creative" and live life on your own artistic path.

Choquette, Sonia. *Your Heart's Desire: Instructions for Creating the Life You Really Want*. New York: Random House, 1997.
- This book covers nine universal, spiritual principles for transforming your life.

Gandy, Debrena Jackson. *All the Joy You Can Stand: 101 Sacred Power Principles for Making Joy Real in Your Life*. New York: Random House, 2000.
- This is a guide on how to practice joy and experience renewal in all aspects of your life.

Grabhorn, Lynn. *Excuse Me, Your Life Is Waiting: The Astonishing Power of Feelings*. Charlottesville, VA: Hampton Roads, 2000.
- This book covers the importance of "energy" and how your feelings about and awareness of it affect every aspect of your life.

Greene, Bob. *Make the Connection: Ten Steps to a Better Body and a Better Life*. New York: Hyperion, 1996.
- This is a 10-step exercise program from Oprah Winfrey's personal trainer, based on getting to the root of what creates a weight problem in the first place.

Oliver, Stephanie Stokes. *Seven Soulful Secrets for Finding Your Purpose and Minding Your Mission*. New York: Bantam Doubleday, 2001.

- This is a book directed at black women, with good advice for both men and women on how to design a life that lets you be the best you can be.

Vanzant, Iyanla. *Acts of Faith: Daily Meditations for People of Color*. New York: Simon & Schuster, 1993.
- This is a guidebook of daily reflections geared to blacks on issues that touch on caring for both the self and the community.

Walker, Marcellus A., and Kenneth B. Singleton. *Natural Health for African Americans: The Physicians' Guide*. New York: Warner Books, 1999.
- In this book, medical doctors and other experts give advice on mainstream approaches and natural therapies for good health.

Web Sites

For Job Hunting

www.careerbuilders.com
- This job-hunting Web site has a search engine, advice, and articles.

www.careerjournal.com
- This is the Web site of the *Wall Street Journal*, which provides daily articles, a tool kit for job hunting, discussion boards, a diversity section, and salary and hiring information.

www.careermag.com
- On this site, you can find job tips, include a photo with your posted resume, use a free Web site, and receive automatic matches of your resume with job postings.

www.diversitycareers.com
- This site specializes in jobs in engineering and technology, and includes news on minority career issues and a calendar for minority job fairs.

www.hotjobs.com
- This site provides job search information, resume posting, "hot job" categories, resume templates to help you create your own, and a free Web page for resumes.

www.monster.com
- On this site, you can post your resume, maintain a job search list, get information about benefits, and receive free newsletters.

www.multiculturaladvantage.com
- This site provides articles, resume posting, and job searches; it also includes information on scholarships, grants, and fellowships.

www.naacpjobfair.com
- This site gives information on job fairs around the country, posts resumes, and carries job searches.

www.thingamajob.com
- This site has a search engine for recruiters, job search information, resume samples, interviewing tips, and a career center.

www.workplacediversity.com
- On this site, you can post your resume and search for a job, find diversity news (sorted by minority group membership), and locate diversity organizations and employers.

For Information on the Law

www.eeoc.gov
- This federal government Web site includes instruction on filing EEOC charges, mediation, and an overview of laws.

www.eeolaw.com
- This site provides articles, resume postings, and job searches, and also includes information regarding scholarships, grants, and fellowships.

www.findlaw.com
- This is a general guide for information on legal resources, including a search engine for finding attorneys.

Other Helpful Web Sites

www.africanamericantherapists.com
- This site offers an online directory of black therapists, sorted by city.

www.africana.com
- This site, called the "Gateway to the Black World," offers news, history, articles, and opinions.

www.bet.com
- This is the official Web site of the cable network, and provides searches, chat rooms, bulletin boards, and information on various life issues, including careers.

www.black-collegian.com
- Billed as "career site for students and professionals of color," this site offers articles, information on graduate schools and military opportunities, and allows job searching and the posting of resumes.

www.blackenterprise.com
- This is an online guide to wealth building, finance, career, and small business opportunities.

www.everythingblack.com
- This site has different sections on arts and humanities, business, events, organizations, news, and reference material.

www.javanoir.com
- This is a guide to African American resources on the Internet.

www.littleafrica.com/resources/organizations
- This site has good networking information, including an online professional directory and list of black Web sites.

www.oprah.com
- This is you-know-who's Web site, with articles, tips, and message boards on how to live a richer and more defined life.

INDEX

■

More Justice, More Peace

The Black Person's Guide to the American
  Legal System
Nedra D. Campbell
Lawrence Hill Books, $14.95 (CAN $22.95)
1-55652-468-4

*"From what your rights are, to criminal pro-
ceedings, to how to protect your copyright,
to consumer protection,* More Justice, More
Peace *is an invaluable reference tool for any black person dealing with the
law. Written in clear, understandable language, it explains the rules of the
system that we all should know."*
—TAVIS SMILEY, host of *The Tavis Smiley Show*, NPR

*"Nedra Campbell has written a valuable handbook and guide to navigat-
ing the legal system—most valuable to those most likely to be victimized
by it."*
—JULIAN BOND, chairman, NAACP

The Colors of Love

The Black Person's Guide to Interracial
  Relationships
Kimberly Hohman
Lawrence Hill Books, $14.95 (CAN $22.95)
1-55652-467-6

*"The fight against racism is waged many ways.
This book tells the tale of people who challenge
it one person and one relationship at a time.
The development of a human ethic that embraces the human spirit in all
its variety will emerge from their example."*
—CAROL MOSELEY BRAUN